BECOMING
Beautiful

A Personal Journey Towards Happiness

KARI ROMEO

BALBOA.
PRESS

A DIVISION OF HAY HOUSE

Copyright © 2018 Kari Romeo.

All rights reserved. No part of this book may be used or reproduced by any means, graphic, electronic, or mechanical, including photocopying, recording, taping or by any information storage retrieval system without the written permission of the author except in the case of brief quotations embodied in critical articles and reviews.

Balboa Press books may be ordered through booksellers or by contacting:

Balboa Press
A Division of Hay House
1663 Liberty Drive
Bloomington, IN 47403
www.balboapress.com
1 (877) 407-4847

Because of the dynamic nature of the Internet, any web addresses or links contained in this book may have changed since publication and may no longer be valid. The views expressed in this work are solely those of the author and do not necessarily reflect the views of the publisher, and the publisher hereby disclaims any responsibility for them.

This book is a work of non-fiction. Unless otherwise noted, the author and the publisher make no explicit guarantees as to the accuracy of the information contained in this book and in some cases, names of people and places have been altered to protect their privacy.

The author of this book does not dispense medical advice or prescribe the use of any technique as a form of treatment for physical, emotional, or medical problems without the advice of a physician, either directly or indirectly. The intent of the author is only to offer information of a general nature to help you in your quest for emotional and spiritual well-being. In the event you use any of the information in this book for yourself, which is your constitutional right, the author and the publisher assume no responsibility for your actions.

Any people depicted in stock imagery provided by Getty Images are models, and such images are being used for illustrative purposes only. Certain stock imagery © Getty Images.

Print information available on the last page.

ISBN: 978-1-9822-1146-2 (sc)
ISBN: 978-1-9822-1148-6 (hc)
ISBN: 978-1-9822-1147-9 (e)

Library of Congress Control Number: 2018910407

Balboa Press rev. date: 08/30/2018

Our habitual concepts of beauty come from
how we think people perceive us.

It is an outward view, an external concept.

Over a lifetime of experience, I have come
to realize that beauty is internal.

It comes when we learn to love ourselves, which
creates a feeling of internal happiness and peace.

Our beauty has nothing to do with how others see us
and everything to do with how we see ourselves!

CONTENTS

PREFACE

Defining the Journey

I like myself. I really do. This simple statement is a big deal. You see, for years, more likely decades, I didn't like myself. I felt lacking in some way, the proverbial not enough syndrome.

I considered myself okay looking, a bit chubby, and somewhat deficient in know-how on most of life's subjects. In other words, I was normal.

I have come to realize most people feel insufficient or less than in some way. I have met incredibly beautiful women who thought they needed serious improvement, whether it be in their looks, their abilities, or their smarts. I have met many men who are so talented yet self-deprecating, which frequently shows up through humor.

From where I am today, I must ask, why? Why can't we celebrate our unique beauty? We are all beautiful in ways that are all our own, yet most of us can't see it.

Here is why I think so many of us can't believe in our own beauty. If we cannot feel beautiful on the inside, our outward perceptions of beauty become warped. From my understanding and experience, I believe inner joy has a direct impact on outer beauty. This concept doesn't have anything to do with makeup or clothing choices. It has everything to do with loving ourselves and appreciating how wonderful we really are.

My current understanding is not something I came up with overnight. In fact, it took decades to finally realize I am solely in charge of how I think of myself and what I consider to be beautiful.

I feel inner happiness is greatly hampered by misguided or limiting beliefs we tend to develop at an early age. These limiting beliefs can form without our knowledge because of the meaning we give early experiences.

I grew up believing I was invisible or not noteworthy because I was the third child of a disintegrating marriage. Mind you, I didn't walk around yelling, "Hey, you, notice me!" Instead, I struggled with a sense of self-worth for much of my adult life. That was but one of the stories I subconsciously told myself.

I have a friend who consistently feels she is a burden to others because her mother used to start statements about what she wished she could do by saying, "If I didn't have children …"

Each of us has stories that have affected us in negative ways. By bringing light to our subconscious-limiting stories, we can make new choices and open our worlds in wonderful ways.

I am writing my story because it took me years to understand I was not only in charge of but responsible for the stories I tell myself. Once I got that, I began to recognize just how limiting my stories were. I also realized these stories and beliefs made my life much harder than it needed to be.

Perhaps through my story you will come to recognize your own limiting beliefs and discover your power to change them. Maybe my story of transformation will inspire you to start your journey of self-discovery. Feel free to use my story and the questions it inspires to help shorten your personal journey toward happiness. We are meant to live fulfilling and joyful lives. I know that now. I wish I had known it when I was younger!

Several years ago, I began the process of learning to like myself. It started with an inner tug to be something more than what I thought I was at that moment.

We all have the tug. We are designed to be evolving creations. There is nothing in our DNA that is designed to be stagnant, although many of us make a darn good attempt at doing just that.

I know that I did. I was safe and secure in what I perceived to be the status quo. I was just fine, thank you very much, letting the world dictate what was right to wear, what was good to say, and even how to act in various situations. I would love to say I was alone in this stagnation, but alas, this is a common malaise in our society. I might even suggest it is an epidemic fueled by expectation, media, and fear.

The media bombards us, showing ideals and standards most people simply can't achieve. We are constantly asked to compare ourselves to others through advertising, television, and social media. The images of happy, beautiful, wealthy, and adventurous people have become a habitual lens through which many view their worlds. Even now, I can spend an hour on Facebook with no effort only to discover everyone seems to be on vacation except me! It is so easy to forget that people don't post about slogging to work every day or taking care of an elderly mother. No, they post the fun stuff. Our brains make an arbitrary decision that everyone else has it better than we do. What I have come to realize and now know for sure is that media, in any form, is one giant illusion.

My theory is that when we are happy inside, it reflects as beauty outside. As I started to put together the threads that became this book, I thought about people I considered truly beautiful. One of the first people I thought of was a woman named Rosemary, a friend of my mother's when I was a young girl. She was a large lady. Her figure would not be considered even remotely ideal. She liked herself, however, and dressed in elegance and style. She applied her makeup tastefully and never left the house without looking like a million bucks. Her preparations all helped, of course, but what made her beautiful were her smile and a certain glow to her. She was happy. She had a solid spiritual foundation.

She had a job she was passionate about, and her family was her world. I can still picture her. She was simply quite beautiful to me. And it wasn't her physical beauty that attracted me. It was the whole package, inside and out.

Recently, I met another woman who reminded me of my mother's friend. Her name is Linda, and while she certainly is blessed in the gene pool, it is her spirit that makes her so spectacular. She dresses with style and moxie (which, incidentally, is the name of her company). She, too, never leaves the house without looking her best. She has a business she is passionate about and a family she adores. She is deeply happy. Linda honors the fact that she is her Lord's creation and lives up to the magnificence with which she was created. She lives her life in service to her family, her business, her church, and her clients.

Linda believes that when we discover our beauty and live in it, we will be better able to serve others because our focus will be outward rather than inward. When we no longer struggle with self-worth, we are in better positions to be present for our families, coworkers, friends, and others with whom we might interact. She is an absolute pleasure to be around because she radiates joy. She exemplifies whole beauty, inside and out. Linda helped me on my journey to love and embrace my unique self. I am grateful to her for reminding me that what makes me unique makes me uniquely beautiful.

In case you see a theme here about inner joy and spirituality, you are right. This theme is a far cry from religion or dogma. To me, the inner journey of discovery is a journey of the spirit.

While I talk about this in a future chapter, I want you to be comfortable reading this book, so I address spirituality briefly here. I'll introduce some new concepts that will be explored more fully later in the book.

In a nutshell, I feel that when we truly begin to see, feel, and believe that we are unique yet part of a greater whole, our worldviews change. We develop more love and compassion.

Digging into the inner workings of our lives and our places in the larger scheme of things open new possibilities and new responsibilities. No more can I think of just myself. As I am part of a greater whole, I must consider how I serve the whole. This shift in perspective is what the spiritual path is all about for me. It was—is—also my path toward happiness and beauty.

What does it mean to be happy? What does it look like to be beautiful? Both questions could fill a warehouse with books. If you consider some of the things we say, maybe there is an answer there.

Have you ever heard that brides and pregnant women are always beautiful? Why? Because they are usually happy. How we feel about our looks and what others think are completely subjective. However, no matter what we physically look like, if we are fundamentally happy, we glow. Our spirit shines through, and it is magical. Our inner joy gives us a vitality, and that brightness cannot be denied.

The big question is how do we get there? How do we uncover our natural light for all the world to enjoy? That is an individual journey as unique as you are. Telling my story could help you start to uncover some of the limiting beliefs and negative stories you may have that contribute to dampening your light and rob you of your joy. The good news is once you see them, you can change them.

Let's get started by exploring the dictionary's definition of *beauty*. One day I want to find out where the writers of the dictionary got all their definitions, but that is a tale for another book. For now, let's check out the Google dictionary's definition of *beauty*.

> The quality or aggregate of qualities in a person or thing that gives pleasure to the senses or pleasurably exalts the mind or spirit.

My interpretation of this definition says that beauty is in the eye of the beholder. It is completely subjective. I am sure you can think of a time you saw something you thought was amazing, while a friend or family member thought you were nuts. Let me give you an example.

I remember going on a tour of the Vatican Museum in Rome with a group of military personnel and their spouses. At the time, I served as an air force captain stationed in Naples, Italy. The event was one of the benefits I enjoyed while serving and working overseas.

To put this tale in perspective, you must understand that from the first moment you enter the Vatican Museum, there is art everywhere: floor, walls, and ceiling. It is overwhelmingly beautiful. The tapestries, the sculptures, and even the flooring speak of such talent translated into objects that will be enjoyed for centuries!

I enjoy beautiful things. I stepped through the door, turning in my ticket after waiting a few hours in line. My reaction? I cried. I wept at the sheer beauty of the place.

Later that night, at our event dinner, we talked about the museum. I was stunned to hear one of our participants exclaim, "It was the most boring place I have ever been." My reaction was disbelief. Boring? How could that be?

She lamented that she didn't see what the fuss was about. It was just a bunch of paintings. She went on to question what the big deal was about the fingers touching in the middle of the Sistine Chapel ceiling? (The center of the ceiling painting depicts God's finger touching Adam's finger.) I was so stunned by her perception of this remarkable place. How on earth could she think this?

Years later, I have come to realize that the point is beauty is subjective, and sometimes the eye of the beholder is missing a perception gene. (Okay, maybe not, but beauty in the eyes of the beholder sees things differently than I may see them.)

I looked on the internet for other definitions of *beauty*, looking for more interesting and perhaps more useful thoughts. Here are a few I particularly liked.

> There is no definition of beauty, but when you can see someone's spirit coming through, something unexplainable, that's beautiful to me. (Liv Tyler)

> Beautiful is the woman who knows people, places, and things don't define her. She is defined by her acts of loving kindness and a generous heart. (Author unknown)

> Beauty is the enemy. We try to conquer not feeling beautiful all our lives. It's a battle that can't be won. There's no definition of beauty. The only way to achieve beauty is to feel it from inside without breaking down into individual physical attributes. (Miley Cyrus [well said, Miley])

> Beauty is a very complete thing that can't be put in a cage or defined by rules. It doesn't have to be within the parameters that society dictates. My definition of beauty is without rules. It can be the face of a beautiful 90-year-old woman that is full of stories and emotion. Beauty is what somebody's eyes communicate. (Penelope Cruz, *Elle Canada*)

Beauty, it would seem, comes from the heart, not from the physical experience. What I want to convey is that we are all beautiful, even when we don't yet personally see it. Our life experiences are designed to help us come to a place of acceptance, inner peace, and joy, which translates to being happy. For me, it took a long time. Make no mistake, I am still working on it. But

I think I am a much prettier woman today than I was ten, twenty, or even thirty years ago because today, I am at peace with myself. I am happy, and it shows.

As you capture your inner happiness, it will surprise you how many people will ask you, "What's changed?" They will comment on how bright you look. "Did you change your hair?" You can smile and say, "Nope, just got happy!"

On that happy note, why don't we define *happiness*. Warning: *Happy* is just as subjective as beauty, therefore, difficult to define.

The Google dictionary I checked had three definitions. The first definition I find interesting because it was declared "obsolete."

This definition of happy was "good fortune: prosperity." Apparently, someone pointed out that money can't buy happiness, so this definition no longer holds true.

The second definition is more to my liking. It notes that happiness is "(a.) a state of well-being and contentment: joy and (b.) a pleasurable or satisfying experience."

The third definition is more appearance based on the example of "striking happiness of expression."

To address the first definition, it certainly seems easier to be happy when one does not have to struggle financially. However, there are a great many tragically sad rich people in this world, so I suspect money is not the issue here. I do enjoy having sufficient funds to play, give, and experience my world. However, this is not what gives me my inner joy.

The story in these pages is about how I came to my state of well-being and contentment. It took a lifetime of experiences to bring me to a place where I desperately wanted to figure out how to find inner joy and contentment. In fact, it was really when I began to search for what would give me personal peace and joy that my life began to transform in amazing ways.

This journey has not always been easy. Certainly, it has been helped along by outer clues and events. My path was sometimes bumpy, and I was convinced on multiple occasions that I had made a wrong turn. A defining moment for me was when in frustration, I turned to a yoga teacher I had and said I didn't know where to put my focus. It all seemed to be calling my name. She smiled and said softly, "Kari, the journey is the focus." My first thought was that this line would make a great title to a book I should write. The second thought was a bit of an aha moment that changed my perspective from frustration to curiosity. (Here's a clue for your journey, by the way, so you might want to read it again or highlight it).

I love that the word *joy* is thrown into the definition (second definition of *happy*) as I truly believe when we are happy, we are in a state of joy, and joy feels good. Happiness to me is when I am at peace with my world, no matter what is going on around me. This creates a quality in me that others see as beauty. Finding my inner peace and the joy that comes with it are worth the effort.

My journey took me through some of the messiness of life. It included the subsequent self-doubt, self-loathing, and minimal self-worth—feelings that are quite common when we deal with our messy lives.

Don't get me wrong; I have had an amazing life overall. It was how I viewed myself in this amazing life that determined my sense of worth and value. It was my perspective that affected my beauty and my happiness.

I would love to say I figured out my significance, or my necessary place, in the world when I was young, but I did not. What I have come to realize is that life would be utterly boring if we were born in the know and didn't need to experience anything to grow.

Fortunately, we are not designed this way. There are so many factors that affect how we view ourselves in this world. That is precisely what makes each of us unique and sets us on our personal and necessary journeys to become and reach our amazing potentials.

I heard an analogy of a roller-coaster ride to describe our lives.

The roller coaster is exciting because of the ups and downs, twists and turns. If we didn't want the thrill, we would take the little choo-choo express that circles the amusement park, barely traveling fast enough to feel the movement. Boring! No, we want to experience life. And experience is what we get from birth to death. It is what we do with the experience that defines us. For the record, I hate roller-coaster rides. Love life; hate roller coasters. I see absolutely no point in being terrorized for three to four minutes. The analogy still holds, however.

What launched my desire to write my journey toward happiness is that I kept running into people, mostly women, who struggled with their joy and happiness and, of course, their sense of personal beauty. That struggle was prompted by how they felt about themselves and their value in the world. The undercurrent of not being enough is so prevalent in our society that it affects all areas of our lives.

We are enough, however, and so much more. We just need to believe it and then move forward without fear toward what our hearts are calling. We need to realize that life is happening *for* us, not *to* us.

I recently heard a speaker say that life is happening *through* us, which I thought was terrific. This shift in perspective took me from playing the helpless victim to empowerment. As you can imagine, this shift in perspective is much easier said than done. As I was moving through this transformation, it occurred to me that perhaps my tale might assist others to embrace their magnificence and grab the joy that is available to us every day.

My life is composed of the ordinary interspersed with the extraordinary. I am no different than you. I am not an Olympic athlete or a pop star. While I don't lack for much, I wouldn't call myself wealthy. In no way can I say I am even remotely famous. Nope, I am just me. I am, however, passionate about helping people find their happy places. I believe our world can become extraordinary if people like you and I can get happy. What I know for sure is that happiness and beauty are interlinked and absolutely possible for everyone!

To give you a bit of perspective: at this writing I am in my mid-racing-toward-late fifties. The last few years of my life have been a little daunting as I have been stepping out of my comfort zone and into my joy. I changed careers, decided to start investing in myself, and started following my intuition instead of what was expected of me.

While this has not been easy, it has been liberating and resulted in an inner peace that still surprises me. In truth, my spiritual, inner journey began in my late forties. That's when I started following the longing in my heart for something more than racing through life toward the next achievement.

What I ask you now is, Why wait to be happy? Why struggle when you don't have to? There is an alternative. It all starts with you embracing your magnificence and loving yourself.

As you continue reading, you'll read how I discovered the origins of some of my most insidious limiting beliefs. I also tell how I discovered all the best parts of myself and turned those discoveries into a life well lived. Maybe this will inspire you to discover little gems of wisdom to help you step into a life of joy, happiness, and yes, beauty.

Let's take a moment to talk about the structure of this book and how I hope you might use it.

Most of the time people are careful with their books, not wanting them to get dirty or wrinkled. One of my mentors and inspirations is Hal Elrod, an author of multiple books, most notably, *The Miracle Morning: The Not-So-Obvious Secret Guaranteed to Transform Your Life (Before 8 AM)*. His philosophy is that a book should be devoured and become a resource. What he suggests—and I am a big proponent of this—is to highlight meaningful passages, scribble notes in the margins, and have a journal nearby to capture thoughts, feelings, and inspirations.

When you read meaningful books—such as self-development, self-transformation, and self-growth books—having them marked up with what hit you square between the eyes helps you go back and find meaningful data again and again. The book goes from being something to collect dust on a shelf to a resource to return to on each step of your journey. You might notice the category of books I mentioned all start with "self." There is a theme here.

I suggest that you find a highlighter, pen or pencil, and perhaps a journal and get started. At the end of each chapter are questions to ponder. Whether you choose to answer them is entirely up to you. This book is also meant to entertain, so if that is all you want, terrific. My promise is that when you let go of the fears that have been holding you back, learn to love yourself, and get happy, you will know a new beauty that feels terrific on the inside and glows on the outside.

Questions to Ponder

What makes you truly happy?

_____

_____

_____

_____

_____

Describe a time when you felt truly happy.

_____

_____

_____

_____

_____

What makes you feel beautiful?

_____

_____

_____

_____

_____

Describe a time when you felt truly beautiful.

_____

_____

_____

_____

_____

What keeps you from feeling happy and/or beautiful?

_____

_____

_____

_____

_____

CHAPTER 1

My Family Backdrop

Any transformation story worth its salt needs a beginning, so I will start with the family into which I was born. That is where most of us start, right? Some of this information is hearsay I picked up in conversations with various family members and friends. This is interspersed with my perceptions of what happened in my youth. Keyword is *perception*.

Even though I view my childhood as sometimes challenging, I still consider myself truly blessed. I was born into a solidly middle-class family in America, meaning I had a roof over my head, food on the table, and reasonable assurance of an education and a chance in life. In other words, I had it way better than many people. With that said, my family also set the stage for a lifetime of feeling invisible, not worthy, and needing to please or fix everyone.

I also start my story by explaining that my family was like most families. There were good times and less good times. We had fights and laughter; I have interspersed stories throughout this book that highlight both. As an adult, I began to reflect on my belief patterns. These patterns were the combination of my childhood events that formed them. To write every event would be unnecessary and, I suspect, boring. Instead, I highlight examples that demonstrate where I suspect my limiting beliefs took shape.

1

To help you understand why I had the perception of being invisible, it is important to understand my parents' marriage and what state it was in when I arrived. It was still going relatively strong, although I suspect strained by the time I was born. Mom and Dad grew up in post-Depression-era families and were young during World War II. Those two events shaped their family dynamics.

Their parents were hardworking, disciplined survivors. As a result, there was, as I understand it, not much demonstrative love. My parents loved each other to the best of their abilities, but by the time I was old enough to understand, it just didn't seem like they had a love affair. I can't recall my father ever telling my mother he loved her. I think they liked each other well enough, but I don't know if love was much a part of the equation.

My family could be called moderately dysfunctional. As there doesn't seem to be a comprehensive instruction manual for raising kids or staying married, I have come to understand that most people's families are moderately dysfunctional. To say I suffered would be an untruth, however. If you ask me if I flourished in my childhood, I would have to say categorically no. Let me set the stage for the family dynamics I found when I arrived on the scene.

My father was a military man. He was navy through and through. He was a pilot, and like many navy men of the pre-Vietnam era, he was often gone for extended periods. When they go on a ship tour, they deploy for six to nine months or longer. Dad was no exception. I am not sure if Dad minded these extended absences because he loved to fly. But his absences left my mom to deal with three kids basically on her own.

I have two older siblings. My sister is a few years older than me, and my brother is a few years older than her. My brother was what mothers call a handful. He was hyperactive and into everything. Mom was overwhelmed with just him.

Before my sister and I came along, our family lived near a military base. It was the late fifties, and the military spousal community was much different than it is now. Military wives had the same rank as their husbands back then. My father was an officer, so Mom was expected to perform as an officer's wife. She never really fit that mold. Mom was an overwhelmed single mother for all intents and purposes in an environment where it was simply frowned on to struggle or fail. Her parents held to the notion that since she was married, it was her husband's responsibility to help. While they did assist some, Mom felt out of place and all alone.

Making the situation worse was the fact that my father could be far less than sensitive at times. It is simply the truth. He could at times be amazingly generous, and at other times, he was impossible. (He passed away several years ago, God rest his soul.) If Mom turned the heat up, he followed behind and turned it down. I am certain he did that to be ornery. There are so few military pilots, and their training is arduous and expensive. Some of them hold themselves in very high regard. I suspect my dad was one of those. He could be obnoxious and arrogant or kind if he chose. Additionally, he and my mom drank like fish. They were smart, but neither knew how to communicate with each other. They also didn't understand what a loving relationship looked like.

Mom was depressed and frustrated at least part of the time. Unfortunately, she turned to alcohol. Not on purpose, of course, but it proved a good relaxer after chasing my brother around and trying to appear socially acceptable to the world. Before long, my sister came on the scene. She was born on my dad's birthday, while he was gone yet again. He thought it was a pretty good birthday gift.

Mom loved her children and did the best she could. She says she has always been socially awkward, but I suspect the truth is my mom is intelligent but has no filter when she speaks her mind. She is a voracious reader and, as such, knows things. She always has some bit of wisdom to impart. Back in the days of Vietnam, social pecking orders, and dressed-up cocktail parties, broaching subjects like politics and communism was frowned upon. Mom couldn't discuss the difficulties she had coping with her kids either. Nor could she discuss her growing depression. Mother felt isolated, frustrated, and at times, helpless. Alcohol helped, at least in her mind.

Eventually, I showed up on the scene. Dad was still gone quite a bit and had moved up in rank. Mom was still trying to make a life for us while drowning. I should also include one more relevant detail. Mom and Dad grew up in strict families and lacked demonstrative love. Mom, as the oldest of three girls, was expected to work just as hard as her mother. who never sat down. My maternal grandmother was truly one of the sweetest women I ever met. She never seemed to stop, however, whether baking cookies, sewing, or cleaning. My paternal grandfather was the strong, silent type; there is no doubt that he ruled the roost. Mom liked to read, which is hard to do when you are trying to emulate an energizer bunny (namely my grandmother, who we incidentally referred to as Momma Bunny).

The house my father grew up in was pretty much loveless. My paternal grandparents loved each other, but it was a sensible love. You showed your love by ensuring there was food on the table, clothes on the children, and going to church on Sunday because God should get some attention at least once a week. I am guessing my father was seldom hugged as he had a real tough time giving hugs. I throw this part in here now because, by the time I was born, Mom and Dad were at the point they didn't even like each other very much. Their relationship morphed into a tolerated friendship if you will. Mom was pretty much a solid alcoholic by then. It wasn't pretty. Dad was an alcoholic as well, although he never admitted it.

Dad attained the rank of lieutenant commander but never advanced any farther. Having served and knowing what I do about old-time spousal politics, I suspect Mom's drinking may have played a role in the cessation of his promotions. That was one side of the coin. The other was that my father was a crass man with no idea how to show appreciation. His humor could be cruel. He, like my mother, was socially awkward. He liked to hang out with his pilot buddies and drink, a lot. This combination didn't bode well for the overall dynamics of military promotions. Whatever the reason, Dad received no more promotions and decided to leave active duty and go into the reserves. The result of this was that when I was four, we packed up and moved from California to Washington.

Dad still wasn't around much. He worked a lot during the week and went flying many weekends. Again, this left Mom alone to deal with three small kids on her own. My older brother was into everything, broke pretty much everything, and was what some might call, hell on wheels. His heart was big, but he was nonstop! Mom didn't know about allergies or ADHD/ADD. All she knew was that she was tired. My sister was a good girl and, therefore, easier to handle.

As for me, I just was. I didn't like conflict even then, so I was mostly quiet and tried to make peace if there was upset in the house. I felt invisible. I started my quest to prove my worthiness quite early because I felt so unseen in my home. Keep in mind this is a child's perception. We pick up crazy beliefs when we are children and frequently don't realize it until much later in life.

This situation set me up to become a lifelong fixer. I needed to fix what and who I perceived as broken regardless of whether the object—people or situations—wanted to be fixed or thought they were broken in the first place. Being a fixer was useful in our house because my mom was always trying to be gracious and serving to those in need. As a result, we frequently had other people living with us.

My aunt and her two children stayed with us for a few years. I shared my room with my cousin. Somewhere in that time we also took in a young man close to my brother's age. At one point, we took in a family whose house had burned down. It was chaotic with never a dull moment. I had to fight for attention even more, and helping others became the way to get noticed. I have to say that despite the chaos, I learned service from Mom, even though some of her efforts were misplaced.

Vietnam happened, and Dad, once again, was gone. He did back-to-back nine-month tours, coming home for only a brief time between. During that time, Mom decided she had a problem and knew she needed to do something about it. I was eight at the time. I was very grateful for Alcoholics Anonymous (AA) because they saved my mom. It is a powerful thing to be so young and watch your mom go through detox with no real way to help her. I remember her shaking so vividly. I held her arm and tried to comfort her. I am tremendously proud of her because she kicked the alcohol and never went back to it. She even quit smoking at the same time. She did this with little help from her family, community, or even her church as those kinds of problems were personal back then. Thank goodness it is okay to ask for help now. Thank goodness there is not such a social taboo on having an illness. And make no mistake, addiction is an illness.

Mom and Dad's tenuous relationship deteriorated more because of a variety of things, but I suspect the inequality in drinking habits played a large part. Dad was a heavy drinker, and Mom was hanging on to sobriety. AA has a funny side effect. When people attain sobriety, they feel so much better, they want everyone else to feel that way too. Recovering alcoholics can be pretty annoying as they set out to save all their booze buddies from sure destruction. While their hearts are in the right places, their salvation efforts are sometimes not welcome. I now understand the addict must first realize he or she is an addict before making any meaningful change. No matter who or how many inform the addict of the problem, it is the personal realization that sets the stage for the recovery process to begin.

Mom didn't get that in the early stages of her sobriety. Or

perhaps she did but carried on bravely anyway to help Dad get sober. I even remember an intervention Mom organized for Dad. She invited his mother, neighbors, and all us kids. We told him our concerns and lovingly asked him to quit drinking. It didn't go over well. Grandma was clearly not fully on board with this intervention as she took Dad to lunch afterward and bought him some wine.

Regardless of family challenges, Mom and Dad ensured we were clothed, had an annual vacation, and went to a good school. When I was in third grade, all three kids changed schools to attend a small, nondenominational parochial school. While I had some challenges at this school, I am still grateful as the education there was better than at the public schools in our area. I am even more grateful to my parents as I now realize this must have been a huge financial burden. Nothing like adding financial stress to an already stressed out marriage.

The bottom line is that my childhood was a mix of confusion, stress, some humor, and little to no demonstrative love. Although I felt invisible, I knew at my core that I was loved. Small moments and events throughout my childhood let me know that in their way, my parents loved me. Daily life in our house was one of getting by without a grandiose argument, people storming out the door, or palpable tension. My parents should have gotten divorced when I was about ten, but they stayed together for the kids. It's my opinion that this was not a good idea. My sister and I have discussed our family situation numerous times as we struggled with our own failed relationships. We now understand that we never had a role model of what love could look like, of how to communicate with a spouse, or even how to create a happy home.

My family backdrop created childhood perceptions that made me think if I were prettier or smarter, maybe I would be noticed more. I went to great lengths to get noticed. A goofy example of this occurred when I was about ten. We were doing construction on a deck, and my sister stepped on a nail. Well, you might think the world had come to an end. She was lavished (at least in my mind) with attention as she was whisked to the doctor for a tetanus shot. She got a lollipop from the doctor too. What did I do? Stepped on a nail of course … by choice! I, too, went to the doctor. My attention, however, was a good talking to and no lollipop.

My point is that I grew up believing I wasn't special. I didn't think I was smart enough, cute enough, or anything enough to be noticed. I did what I could to draw any attention to myself. The nail story might add relevance to my perceived intelligence. Hey, I was young and desperate for attention. It took decades to find my truth, which is that I am smart, beautiful, and a necessary essence of our world. I had to let go of many limiting beliefs to get to that realization. The result of liberating myself from these beliefs is a freedom that translates to inner joy and outer lightness.

While I understand more today than I did back then, the family backdrop influenced how I related to the world and myself for many years. I know for sure that early childhood, or what is known as the formative years, can greatly affect our beliefs on how the world should work and our places in it. It is important to note, however, that everyone experiences issues and challenges as children. As we get older, we have a choice of how to view those challenges and what to do about them. We have the right and personal responsibility to question and change any limiting beliefs formulated during our childhoods.

I encourage you to dig deep to find hidden limiting beliefs developed along your childhood journey and begin today to change them. As you look at your childhood, perhaps you will recall stories that helped you form less than empowering beliefs. Please, let go of judgment and blame. Instead, find compassion for all the people and events that helped mold you. With compassionate understanding, you will have the courage and wisdom to formulate a new paradigm for yourself. My promise to you is that when you challenge these limiting beliefs, your world will open in wonderful ways.

Questions to Ponder

What significant memories stand out from your childhood?

_____

_____

_____

_____

_____

What limiting beliefs did you form because of these events?

_____

_____

_____

_____

_____

How can you take these limiting beliefs and reframe them today in a more-empowering statement of self?

> Limiting belief example: "If I were prettier, people would like me."

> Empowering belief example: "I am beautiful in my own way, and when I appreciate my beauty, I will be more available to create healthy relationships with others."

_____

_____

_____

_____

_____

CHAPTER 2

My Family Dynamic

Dad didn't have a clue how to show love except to ensure we had clothes on our backs and food on the table. Dad felt deeply responsible for us, and to that end, he was very reliable. I certainly didn't starve, and as the third child, I had my share of new clothes and plenty of hand-me-downs. What I perceived as lacking was a parent who was a champion in my life. Part of this perception was due to my poor self-image. I didn't ask for what I wanted, like participating in activities, so there was not much for my parents to champion. The other side of this story is that for the first time, moms were going to work in droves and, therefore, not home for their kids. It was the early sixties, and this was a relatively new phenomenon. Add a dicey marriage to the mix, and I felt like I didn't stand a chance.

Maybe we have adjusted to the new working norms because when I look at friends who have children, they seem so involved in their children's lives. My sister has a daughter, and she encouraged her to try so many things, from soccer to dance and theater. She even sent her to model school. She supported her when my niece wanted to take up an instrument only to drop it a few years later. The situation doesn't seem to matter; my sister is and always will be the champion of my niece and her development in this world. I help, too, as I am the cool aunt.

In reviewing my childhood, I tried to remember my parents coming to a game or watching me perform. The realization that hit me while on this little tour of memory lane was twofold. First, I only participated in sports one year, and I don't remember my parents coming to see an event. I participated in gymnastics, track, and soccer, so there were plenty of events to choose from. The second memory was that I tried an instrument and was terrible, so that lasted about five minutes.

As far as my parents supporting or encouraging me in my activities, there just weren't any for them to support. I didn't get involved in much of anything. I told Mom a few years ago that I wished I had taken ballet as a kid. She was surprised and wondered why I didn't ask her for lessons. I don't know the answer to that question, but I almost responded by asking her why she didn't get me involved in anything. That would not have been nice.

Mom encouraged art for a while, but that was pretty much it that I recall. I felt like Mom and Dad were in survival mode, and there just didn't seem to be any energy left to encourage me in anything. I suspect if I had pushed to get into extracurricular activities, they would have been okay with that. I didn't, they didn't, and that was that. That sounds horrible, but it is important for my story because I took up the mental mantra that I never felt special and wasn't good at anything. Instead, I grew up being responsible.

We earned our allowance by doing chores around the house. I was a champion dishwasher by the time I left home. Pretty handy with a toilet brush too! Mom was never a particularly good house cleaner, so my sister and I did the housework. Like I said, I grew up responsible.

From an early age, I knew I didn't like conflict, and my household was a proving ground to see if I could help alleviate it. The fixer in me was in my element. I found humor to be a good moderator, so I became the family clown. Sometimes something ridiculous can cause laughter and break the tension. I also have a deep sense of compassion and frequently found myself listening to my mother when she was distressed. My natural compunction was to try to fix things, which as a little girl, just wasn't possible. This desire to make everything right played a pivotal role in blocking true happiness as an adult, at least until I started taking responsibility for my thoughts, choices, and feelings. I get into that later in the book.

Rest assured that I do have happy memories of that time. It was not all bleak. Each member of our family had a unique sense of humor, and as such, we had quite a few laughs. The fact that our front door was a revolving one for people in need also set the stage for some laughter as pranks could create some real humor with so many different players. The young man we took in and my biological brother defined trouble just by being alive. I had to check my bedroom and the bathroom regularly for boobytraps! My aunt left her wig stand in the bathroom once. Not a good idea. She found it later with the face painted like the lead singer from the band KISS. She was not amused, even though the rest of us were!

I fell victim to my brother's pranks on so many occasions. I was pretty gullible as a little girl. I got him back though one evening. He used to sneak out the downstairs door at night. I usually heard him because he was noisy when he came in sometime around one or two in the morning. He would use the bathroom, which was right across from my bedroom. As I am a light sleeper, I always heard him. One night I carefully balanced a plastic container full of water on the top of the door and the door frame. Then I went to my room and pushed my bed up to the bedroom door, so my brother wouldn't be able to get in. I waited with such anticipation.

Sure enough, he opened the bathroom door, and water dumped all over him. I could hear him swearing even with the pillow over my head to drown out my laughter. He tried my door to no effect. He got me back though in such a terrible way. He did not say one word the next day. Not a peep. No acknowledgment at all. He didn't admit that I got him until I was almost forty! I was deeply satisfied the day he finally told me, and we shared a good laugh.

After we arrived in Washington, and for several years after, Mom and Dad made sure we went to church and catechism so that we would have a good Christian foundation for life. I discovered I could be the star of the show in my Sunday school classes by memorizing better than anyone else. I am not sure what happened to my memory as an adult, but as a kid, I was a rock star memorizer. My enhanced memory was because I desperately wanted to be noticed; I wanted to feel special. But the church and later school were poor substitutes for a parent's attention.

I don't remember much about my early years in school, before we went to the parochial school. I suspect I was a bit stubborn though. One day when I was in kindergarten, I showed up at our front door midway through the day. My mother was horrified and asked why I was there. I told her the teacher made me mad. Next, my mother asked how I got home. "I walked, of course," was my reply. To put this in context, it was a two-mile walk that involved crossing a major freeway. Perhaps I had authority issues.

I wonder about those early years because when I was in my twenties, I found a box of school papers and report cards Mom kept. To my horror, I found a letter from a first- or second-grade teacher, telling my mother that I was obviously not getting enough love at home because I was so needy in class. She actually wrote that. It broke my heart, and I called my mom immediately to apologize for the hurt I caused her.

I also gave Mom joy. She didn't have much, so I made it my mission to help her out. A favorite family tale took place during the Ford administration. Betty Ford put on such elegant state dinners. Fine magazines frequently featured her tables. Mom always wanted an elegant table, which was impossible with a bunch of hooligans who comprised our family and houseguests. I took one of those magazine photos and copied it ... after a fashion.

I found an old bedsheet from our youth, stains and all, and dressed the table. I took a pair of ratty, old, pink, fluffy Chewbacca slippers and used them for candleholders. I found every chipped and mismatched plate I could find and set the table. The flatware was a combination of plastic, camping tools, and normal silverware. I topped it off with mismatched candles for the slippers. Finally, for the center I made a tent card that read, "Eat Your Heart Out Betty Ford." I was a very clever child. The family did get a laugh, and I think my mom felt better that day. For the record, we ate at that table that night and perhaps for a few nights after. I was in heaven.

Our dinner table was a never-ending source of irritation for Mom. She wanted to have decorum at the table, but it just didn't happen. For example, she had women over from church one afternoon. She set the children up in one room, and her guests in the formal dining room. We actually did pretty well on our own until dessert was served. She gave us ice cream with blueberries on top. My brother tossed a blueberry at one of our guests' children, and that was what the older ones needed to start a food fight. Before long, ice cream and berries were everywhere. Mom didn't stand a chance in hell of having elegance with us around. Maybe we were all looking for attention.

One evening we took things a little too far for even Mom! It was a night with just us three kids, Mom, and Dad. I believe it was my sister who asked my brother a rather obvious yes answer question. My brother retorted with the question, "Does a bear shit in the woods?"

My sister came right back with, "Is the pope Catholic?" This line of discussion went back and forth for a while, with my father laughing, and Mom getting more irritated by the minute. She reiterated that she wanted a nice table, not a circus. Dad didn't help at all as he found it all hilarious.

Right about then, my sister looked my sixteen-year-old brother in the eye. With a straight face she asked him, "Do you have voluntary or involuntary erections?" Dad spit food about twenty feet as he roared with laughter. Mom slammed her plate on to the table so hard it broke and then went to her room. She didn't talk to us for about two weeks. Classic family meal. For the record, my brother did not have a reply!

When I was about ten, around the time we were building the deck, my father walked into our living room and calmly told Mom he was having a heart attack. Mom set a land speed record getting him to the hospital, which the doctors said was the only reason he lived. When Dad came home, everything changed. You see, when you have a heart attack, you immediately lose your pilot's license. Dad's entire identity was as a pilot. He became an angry man, and our household was never the same. Everything irritated him. The tension in the air was palpable. The situation between he and Mom went from bad to worse.

I spent a fair amount of time running interference between them. My brother was gone; he left home around sixteen and never really came back. My sister could drive, so she started working as well as going to school. That left only me at home with the warring parents. Mostly, it was rather like a cold war—a lot of silence and tension. Somehow, I felt I should try to fix things, but there was no fix. I think this cemented my belief that I was not good enough and had to work harder. It is crazy how children can sometimes take on responsibility for their parents' situation when they aren't even old enough to take care of themselves.

I insert this last story about my family because it is a great demonstration of where I felt I fit in the grand scheme of things. My brother's birthday is in April. He is the first. My sister's birthday is on the same day Dad's. Pretty easy to remember both of those. My birthday is in December. For some reason, the family forgot my birthday several times, which certainly added credence to my assertion that I felt invisible. A few times when I realized no one remembered, I made a cake. Mom or Dad would ask, "What is the cake for," and I would answer, "My birthday." What followed were usually several swear words and an apology.

When I was in my thirties, my mom got the bright idea to give everyone in the family a perpetual calendar (one that only had numbers and not the day assigned, so it can be used again and again). She carefully put everyone's birthdays on it, so we could all remember. It included the immediate family, aunts, uncles, and a few other important dates to remember. We all got one for Christmas. My sister thanked Mom and then pointed out that she forgot one birthday. You guessed it … mine. Some things never change.

My family life had some challenges to be sure, but I learned some great life lessons as a result. I did not recognize these lessons until I stopped feeling like a victim and began to look for the benefits my childhood brought me. In retrospect, there are quite a few. For example, my mom helped me become a more compassionate person. I also learned service from her. Both parents helped me become the responsible person I am today. I learned money management and how to get and keep a job from them. I learned that humor could break tension and put people back in to a place where they can communicate. I learned resilience and self-reliance.

The last paragraph is important. You see, many people go through their entire lives blaming a difficult childhood for everything they experience as an adult. Blaming is easy to do. And it is a cop-out that keeps us from facing reality or taking responsibility for our current situations. What I learned as I started digging deeper into my peace of mind is that through gratitude and compassion, we can shift our perspectives to a more positive one. I grew to look at my childhood with a new set of eyes, one in which I have compassion for my parents' situation and gratitude for the better person I became because of them.

Every time a negative memory comes up, I endeavor to look at it through this new lens, and inevitably, my thoughts about the situation improve considerably. This shift took time, and as I mentioned, compassion for my parents and myself. What is interesting to me is that this new perspective has changed the way I look at my childhood overall. Not only that, but as I developed my new viewpoint, the negative memories began to fade. They just didn't hold power over me anymore.

In fact, as I wrote this, my deep dreams became filled with grief. I would dream of crying and mourning but wake up feeling like a million bucks! I believe that as I wrote this book, I was truly and completely letting go of the perceived hurts of my childhood. I can focus now on how fortunate I am that I had so much. I am a fulfilled person because of the lessons I learned as a child. I didn't realize some of those lessons until I was in midlife, however.

I am now caring for my ailing mother. I can see her now with much more clarity. Her sadness and regret for her part in my life are tragic. Mom struggles at times to see the positive. She has no compassion for herself, which makes me sad. She was once a very handsome woman and still is to some degree. But she never considered herself beautiful. Now she frequently seems sad and calls herself horrible names. She says she is too old to learn new ways of being. My message to you is that you can change your perspective if you struggle with a less-than-perfect childhood. It is worth it to let go of pain and embrace gratitude and compassion! Don't wait to embrace healing and forgiveness.

Please understand that everyone had at least some difficulties as children. Our family roller coasters help to shape us to become greater, stronger members of society. How we view these difficulties has a definite effect on our lives as adults. If you have negative memories or bad feelings about your family, I encourage you to change your perspective. Look through the lens of gratitude for the lessons you learned.

There are always lessons to be learned, and if faced head-on, we grow into better people. After gratitude, the second lens to consider is compassion. Can you see the bigger context of the situation or action that caused you distress? Soften your gaze to see the whole of a situation. Compassionate awareness is a great step toward forgiveness and grace. It is not always easy. Some childhood situations are truly horrific. What I suggest, however, is to find the courage to move past your childhood through compassion for yourself and others so that you can live a richer, fuller life now. You have the opportunity to choose how you feel. The power is all yours.

The effort is worth it. Like me, you might even be able to find gratitude for your childhood. This effort will leave you feeling lighter. The negative shadow you might not have even known you had will dissipate, and your beautiful inner light will become brighter. That light is beautiful, and it is meant to shine. Set your beauty free through forgiveness, compassion, and peace.

Questions to Ponder

What is your earliest memory, and how did it influence your life?

_____

_____

_____

_____

_____

What events in your childhood taught you specific lessons?

_____

_____

_____

_____

What, if anything, would you change about your childhood if you could? (For the record, I am not sure that I would. I will only say that I wish I had been involved in more kid-friendly activities. I am not sure I ever learned to play.)

_____

_____

_____

_____

CHAPTER 3

School Sets the Stage

The parochial school I went to included grades 1 to 12, however, I started in the third grade. The school had a good reputation and was noted for small classes, which typically results in more student care from teachers. My teachers were attentive, and I am sure they did their best. Some of these very attentive teachers were also the reasons I developed one of my most insidious limiting beliefs—that I wasn't smart. I liked the school, however, and have some good memories from there. I still remember many of my teachers' names and what they looked like. This is a feat after forty years! Alas, third grade set the stage for my belief that I couldn't do the math, was a poor reader, and wasn't particularly smart. I go into that more in a minute.

I was the last of the three children to join this school. By the time I entered, my brother had left the school, and my sister was still on reasonably good terms. My start at school included having to overcome the reputation of my overly enthusiastic brother. Nothing like a good challenge to start a school career.

Some teachers were more memorable than others. My first teacher had long, thick, beautiful red hair. She was very nice, but her hair was so spectacular, I fear that is all I remember. In all fairness, I was probably eight at the time, so a bit of memory lapse can be forgiven.

Another of my early teachers was a short woman with a tiny waist and larger hips. We were horrible kids because behind her back, we called her Ms. Whalebuns. She had a big heart and loved the kids, which I can only imagine took some doing with such a rambunctious bunch that age group presents. I must throw in a fun story about this teacher. Or more to the point, what I did to her. I had a very good friend, whom I will call Jay. He was the son of another teacher at the school. Jay had a glass eye; he lost an eye as a young boy due to an early childhood illness. He could pop the eye in and out with ease. I thought it was the coolest thing ever. Most of the other girls thought it was super gross.

Jay and I sat in the back of the room, right in front of this teacher's desk. One day while she was at the front chalkboard, putting problems on the board, I asked Jay for his eye. I dropped it in her teacup, which at the time was full of steaming tea. We then waited, trying hard to look innocent and very attentive. With great anticipation, we watched as she headed back to her desk for a sip of tea. Her reaction was marvelous. There was a scream, a thrown teacup, and a half hour spent looking for the eye. The incident was followed by several more hours in the principal's office. Totally worth it.

This poor woman sticks in my mind as a teacher as well because it was in her class that I learned I wasn't as smart as most of the rest of the class. She started giving timed math tests to help us hone our skills. I will tell you that math is not my forte, and I don't particularly like it. I can work math problems just fine, thank you very much, although it takes me some time. I know that now. Then, I was not so sure. My brain needs a fair amount of time to work out the logic of a math problem, which, of course, you don't have with a timed test. I could never finish the darned things.

I ended up in remedial math. As it turned out, I was also not a fast reader. I now think I am mildly dyslexic, but at the time, I just appeared to have trouble reading. As it was a very small school, it was easier to lump all the slower kids in a group. If my memory serves me correctly, I spent my entire experience at this school in the remedial lane. I also graduated from the same school.

My one-eyed friend and I shared many classes over the years. We were both in remedial land and not part of the cool group. It didn't help that we were also somewhat lacking in charm. We were in high school biology with a teacher who was brilliant but spoke in a monotone. It was the first class after lunch, so listening to his voice was brutal. One day, Jay had his head on the table, trying to stay awake. I was dutifully watching the teacher and showing that I was attentive. Although I might have just been hypnotized by that voice, come to think of it. Anyway, Jay burped ... loudly! Without any hesitation, he picked his head up, looked at me, and said, "Gross, Kari!" What are friends for?

By the end of third or fourth grade, I was firmly entrenched in the notion that I was not good in school or particularly smart. My newly found limiting belief was the lens through which I viewed the next eight school years and well beyond. It was not helpful that my sister breezed through school with no effort at all and very near the top of her class. I don't think she even studied! It didn't seem fair. Now, of course, I am super proud of her. At that time, however, I may have had a little resentment.

At this point, it is important to remind you that I was the third of my family to go to this school. My older brother was the first, and although well meaning, he was notorious for his youthful humor, which could at times be rambunctious. His first day at that school, the first-period teacher walked into the room to find him with his feet upon the instructor's desk. Then my brother tossed a plastic hand grenade at the teacher. Did I mention this teacher went on to become the principal? My brother left the school after two years to attend another high school.

My sister, on the other hand, was a straight-A student without trying. She had challenges with some of the teachers, but she was a star student and overcame them. My father felt like she should have been treated better, however, and had a terrible argument with the principal. Dad felt that since the school was very expensive, none of his children should have anything other than smooth sailing through school.

I was doomed. By the time I hit high school, I was following in the wake of my supposedly troublemaking family. Some teachers expected me to be trouble, so they were not supportive at all. One English teacher was not even covert about her dislike for my family. I had to work hard to get anything above a C in her class. She made it very clear that she didn't have time to waste on my family's kids. It was sad because I liked to write and tell stories. Every so often, I have what-if moments, but they serve no purpose except to keep me from the possibility of today and this moment.

I joined the choir in high school. My sister was one of the star singers during her tenure at the school. She had a wonderful, strong voice. I love to sing, but I have what I call a middle-range voice. I sing well enough as long as there is no more than two- or three-note range difference. A song has to be pretty square in the middle register for me to be able to sing it. Too high and I crack. Too low and my voice disappears altogether.

My friends wanted me to participate, however, so I was encouraged to mouth the words but not sing. The teacher didn't argue. It did not take long for me to leave the choir. Again, I wonder what would have happened if I had taken singing lessons like my sister. I still love to sing and do as often as I want now. My range hasn't changed much, but my perception of my ability has. I honor how I sing today, and during the bits I can't do, I use that time to enjoy and appreciate the music of other voices.

I also had some deeply encouraging teachers. My art teacher was named after a cartoon character we all thought was great. He loved teaching and could make the most artistically lacking student feel good about what he or she painted. I had some artistic talent, so his classes were a real pleasure for me. I painted a few things that members of my family still have in their homes. I sometimes wonder what my life would have looked like had I chosen to pursue art instead of work as a means to feel special. I didn't as I still didn't have much self-esteem and, therefore, could not see my talent. But this teacher instilled in me a love of all things beautiful. I can spend hours in a gallery, museum, or even a well laid out kitchen store because I like the design and pretty things.

Mom once wanted to drive me from Seattle to Portland to explore a school for the arts and design. She saw my talent and wanted me to pursue it. I was just not secure enough in myself, so I balked at the possibility and would not go. I can't remember if I ever thanked her for that moment when she tried to do something special for me. The fact I can't remember makes me sad. I must believe now that all these events, both the successful and the misguided, helped me grow into the wonderful woman I am today. Remember at the beginning of this book, I noted that life is sometimes messy.

Another favorite teacher was not a teacher at all but the school janitor. His name was Mr. Hoffsteader. He loved the kids unconditionally. It seemed like anytime someone fell and got a boo-boo, he was there to give comfort. One year he spent much of his meager salary to buy all the younger kids teddy bears. Mine was black and white, and I named him Funky Winkerbean. I loved that dumb bear. I had it for years. When Mr. Hoffsteader died, the school closed to attend his funeral. It was my first funeral, and oh, how I cried. The school was never the same without him. He taught us all the meaning of loving service. I was probably in fifth grade when he died, and now, almost forty years later, I can still clearly picture him in his baggy black pants, wrinkled grayish-white shirt, and suspenders. I can still see Funky Winkerbean too. I had that bear until my early thirties. The bear represented unconditional love and someone who understood how to give it.

While still in high school, I started working in earnest because I learned responsibility growing up in my household. What I discovered was that I could gain a certain independence as well as earn an income. After a few years picking strawberries and blueberries during summers, I got my first real job at Baskin and Robbins Ice Cream. I was sixteen. I don't remember how much I worked there, but I do remember I was not fond of the boss and scooping hard ice cream is much more difficult than it looks. My wrists hurt so badly at the end of the day from scooping Rocky Road ice cream, and I had ice cream all over me. But most of the customers were fun, and I quickly learned that work was a place where I could stand out. I discovered that people—and their dogs—enjoyed being treated like rock stars, and most appreciated good service. I developed a regular clientele and enjoyed the fact that I felt wanted and special because people waited for me to serve them instead of one of my coworkers.

Once I started working, I pretty much forgot anything that happened at school. I honestly cannot remember anything of my junior and senior years. I became solely focused on work. I worked as much as I could weekdays and weekends. It got me out of the house, which in my mind was a very good thing. It also earned me money, and I liked having that particular resource because it gave me options. In retrospect, however, I see that working so much was unfortunate. I did not participate in any of the high school rituals. I never wore a prom dress. I am well versed with restaurant aprons, however.

I now think our school years should be for school. I advocate working summers, but during the school year, I think a kid ought to be allowed to be a kid. My parents didn't force me to work. I did that all on my own. I started actively working in tenth grade and never participated in anything school-like after that. I didn't make friends, and I didn't go to events. I worked. And I loved it because I was important at work. Working provided my one other clue to the direction my life would go. You see, it was at work that I discovered I was born to lead.

Questions to Ponder

What events in your school years taught you specific lessons?

_____

_____

_____

_____

_____

What teachers influenced you and why?

_____

_____

_____

_____

_____

How did your school experience shape your beliefs today?

_____

_____

_____

_____

_____

If so, how do those beliefs now serve your highest purpose?

_____

_____

_____

_____

_____

CHAPTER 4

Leadership and a Relationship for all the Wrong Reasons

I used work to fill the gaps in my psyche. I grew up with the perception of being invisible, but at work, I not only got noticed, I could also shine. My school years imbued me with the notion that I wasn't smart, but at work, I was promoted again and again. You must be smart to be promoted, right? Some situations in my childhood, like my parents' contentious marriage, set me on the road to be a serial mediator and fixer. Being in leadership positions allowed me to be the champion of my employees, which fed my need to fix situations and relationships. Work and leadership were the panaceas for the limiting beliefs that had governed my life so far.

By the time I graduated high school, I was the assistant manager of a Pizza Hut® restaurant. I had just turned seventeen. What I quickly figured out when I started work was that if I performed at a high level, I received attention from pretty much everyone. At that stage in my life, I deeply wanted to be noticed, so I was in my element. Other employees liked working with me because I was a serial people pleaser who loved helping others succeed. My initial positions brought to light my gift of innate wisdom. I always seemed to have the right words to say to help regardless of the situation. People came to me with some conflict or confusion, and I could usually figure out a way for them to work through the problem or approach the relationship from a more balanced point of view. I am also a very positive person, so I was not prone to drama.

I developed a compassionate heart as a young girl. This quality put me in a position to be the one to bring people together when there was a judgment, perception, or even a negative stereotype in play. If a customer was unhappy, I was usually sent to the table to sort out the situation. I was pretty good at turning an angry customer around, but I didn't always succeed.

One evening, a very expensive car pulled into the parking lot. The restaurant boys were all ogling it from the back door of the kitchen. In sauntered a woman and her two young children. Her children were rambunctious and disruptive. I suspect they had insisted she take them to a pizza joint, which was clearly beneath her stratospheric position in life. I also think she must have had some serious insecurity problems as she felt it necessary to put me in my place.

I took them a pitcher of soda earlier and then returned to take their order. For reasons I will never understand, the woman purposely knocked over the soda so that it soiled my uniform. Perhaps she thought it was funny. Her kids certainly did. I was grateful my manager witnessed the event as that was the only reason I kept my job. You see, I cleaned the table and got a new pitcher of soda for this group. As I approached the table, I "tripped" and dumped the entire pitcher in the woman's lap. Her kids thought that was freaking hilarious. I apologized for my clumsiness, of course. My manager quickly took over, and I had to pay for the cleaning of her suit. Totally worth it!

The people pleasing thing also worked out in my manager's favor. Need a job done … give it to Kari. Admittedly, I would get a bit annoyed because I felt picked on at times. I also felt many managers were simply lazy. Working toward management positions myself made me feel special, but it also showed lazy managers what it means to work hard. I am not so sure they noticed or cared. Rather than fix an employee problem, they just got the job done through me. Not that I ever said anything. I had structure, people who noticed me and liked me, and usually recognition through promotion for a job well done. What more could I possibly need?

In fact, I became either the supervisor or the manager at almost every job I have held. I worked hard, and it showed. I usually enjoyed work, but my reasons for working hard were all wrong. I wanted to belong, and I wanted people to notice me. Oh, and I wanted them to like me. I was also fiercely protective of the people who worked for me. I was their champion, cheerleader, and guide.

I look back on all this and realize that I was screaming to be noticed and appreciated. It was also a recipe for disastrous romantic relationships as I also wanted a loving partner. I didn't know what a loving relationship looked like, so I made some incredibly poor partner choices. The work environment can be challenging for a young manager. I sought emotional support from men I worked for and with. Not a good plan, by the way.

I think the average young man is just as scared as girls are of relationships and how to get into them. They are also over the top hormonal, which is like throwing fuel in a fire! Because so many young women are insecure about their value, beauty, and worth, they are easy targets for the classic one-liner, "But I love you so much." We fall for it over and over and over. Then we finally figure out the motive behind that line is usually sex.

I am not going to spend much time on this one because the period between when I was sixteen and twenty-two is just too embarrassing to recount from a relationship point of view. You see, I now know that I am a smart woman. I sure didn't act like it back then. I also know that during those years, my mind did

29

not govern me. I was trying to fill an empty heart. It didn't work because I didn't love myself, and that is where true love begins. After that little bit of wisdom, let's get back to work!

During this time, I was either the assistant manager or manager of several different entities. I worked mostly in restaurants. I could write a whole book on the time I was a server on the graveyard shift at a restaurant called Sambo's. This diner was near numerous bars. The people who came in after the bars closed were usually entertaining and could be generous with their tips, trying to outdo each other after a night of drinking. I made some of my best money from drunks.

Okay, one story. There was a guy who came in every night. His name was JoJo. He could throw his voice. Really! I have no idea how, but it was cool. I would come up to take his order, and he would answer from behind me while sitting in front of me. I truly have no idea how he did this, but he loved to mess with me. He would make the sound of a baby crying from several tables down. It was two in the morning, so this was not to be expected. It was crazy but fun. He was harmless, and he tipped well. Funny though, I always felt I should tip him.

I eventually got tired of waitressing. I tried college directly out of high school, but I had no focus and no idea what I wanted to do. On top of that, I was fairly convinced I wasn't good at school, so why bother? Around the age of twenty-one, I thought maybe cosmetology school would be good. It was artistic and to my knowledge, didn't require math. That seemed like a good plan except that it was expensive, and I couldn't afford it. These were the Reagan years, and one of his great tax plans changed the way waitstaff were taxed. It used to be we were taxed on what tips we declared. Then someone brilliantly figured out that we probably weren't declaring everything we earned. Well, duh!

The new tax plan taxed on a percentage of our table tickets. If a table spent five hundred dollars, I was taxed on 15 percent of that amount, assuming that was what I earned in tips from that table.

The early eighties were a time of financial unrest, and there were very few people who tipped at 15 percent. Waitstaff paychecks took a big hit. I was already financially strapped, and this new tax did not help one bit.

I found myself living on a couch in an apartment with four other people. I couldn't get into cosmetology school because I couldn't get a loan. Why? My father made too much money. I hadn't lived with my dad since I was sixteen or seventeen, and now I was twenty-one about to turn twenty-two. My father always said that if I went to college straight out of high school that he would pay for it. Well, I went one semester and dropped out. He kept his word and would not give me a dime. I was broke, looking at a bleak future, didn't like myself, and started to get into trouble in ways I don't want to revisit. The bottom line was that I was desperate. I even contemplated taking the easy way out and exiting this ridiculous life I found myself in.

I come from a long line of military officers. It occurred to me that if I joined the military, maybe I could get my degree and then get out and get a decent job. The military would help pay for school, so what was four years when I could, in a sense, get school for free. But I had one small problem. I was heavy. Read chubby. Too heavy to pass the air force entrance requirement. I went back again and again, trying to get in. Finally, I went about four days with no food and only drank water. Then I went and took their entrance test, which I had to take before weighing in. I made it! After I passed the test, I went for a hamburger and fries. Best. Damned. Hamburger. Ever!

I had to wait several months to leave, but in May 1983, I boarded a plane heading to San Antonio, Texas, and basic training. My life was about to take a very dramatic turn. Basic training showed me several things. First, it showed me what a family looked like, and oh, did I ever love that.

Basic training brings diverse people together from all over the United States and throws them into a fairly stressful environment.

If we didn't work together, we didn't make it. All these strangers formed bonds and relationships that resembled a tight-knit family. I would even go so far as to say it was fun. Basic training for me was a breeze. I had grown up with discipline and managed very busy restaurants. I was also about four to five years older than most of the crew.

I became the dorm chief, meaning I was dumb enough to raise my hand when the technical instructor (TI) asked if anyone had management experience. I was in heaven, though, because I love helping people succeed. I love helping them find their inner strength and courage. I love teaching. I am a born leader, and I now had thirty-five to forty people looking to me to help them through these crazy few weeks. As a result, I spent an awful lot of time standing at attention while some TI yelled at me for the actions of one of my troops. It was a big game to weed out the crazies, and there were some that needed weeding. I took it all in stride. I even got in trouble a few times, mostly for bursting out laughing at something absurd the TI said that probably wasn't meant to be funny.

Basic training also put me in contact with my first husband, whom I married about a year later. He was impressed with the pretty girl in charge. It felt good to feel wanted and know he thought I was pretty. At this point, I hadn't figured that part out for myself, so I relished the outside input of my value. I was also still looking for the emotional support of a partner in my often stressful leadership position.

I was offered all sorts of jobs when I was at the recruiter's office, but I turned them all down until they offered air traffic control. I thought this job would please my father as he had been a pilot. I honestly didn't give much consideration as to whether *I* wanted the job. It was that needing attention thing again. After basic training, I headed off to technical school for air traffic control followed by my first assignment, which was in the Republic of Panama.

I started my new career as an air traffic controller (ATC) in Central America. I was a tower controller, and all I can say is that ATC is not for the faint of heart. To have responsibility for keeping all those people in the planes safe was terrifying. Some people do this with no concern and such ease. For me, it was a daily exercise in anxiety. I was on a terrible schedule, which was ruinous for my sleep. To make matters seriously intolerable, I lived in a dorm with a roommate, so my sleep was at the mercy of others' consideration, which was usually lacking!

Moreover, I was trying to please a man who was completely confident and moved through everything with ease. I chose Panama because he moved to Panama. This man liked me, though, and I was determined to earn his love. My first clue that this probably was not a great relationship was the fact that I was trying to earn his love. Love should not be the trophy at the end of an acceptance race. The stress began to get to me in the form of skin rashes. My back was a mess. My leading man and I decided to get married one night after a whole lot of alcohol, which is not a recommended way to decide your future life together. I won the trophy, though, and I was getting married!

If we wanted to stay in base housing, we had to commit to one more year on our tour in Panama, which neither of us wanted. Our first year of marriage, therefore, was spent living in separate dorm rooms with roommates. We scheduled our alone time with the cooperation of our roommates, so spontaneity was not on the menu. That living arrangement did nothing to cement the first year of marriage and bonding.

I continued to love the military, while my new husband hated it. That certainly didn't help with marital bonding either. I was eventually medically released from ATC and put into an administrative role. Shortly after that, we left Panama and headed to Sumter, South Carolina. I had a ball as an administrator because I worked with a group of pilots, providing support in keeping their war plans current, setting up their travel, and the like.

They treated me like gold, and I loved it. I was a star performer, appreciated and needed for the mission. I could not have been more thrilled. My husband, however, hated his job, South Carolina, and life in general. Our marriage wasn't doing much better as he worked the night shift, and I worked days. We rarely saw each other. He asked the air force to release him, and to my surprise, they granted his request. I reluctantly asked to be released as well and was turned down. The day I received notice that the air force denied my exit papers changed my life forever.

I told my husband the news over one of our rare dinners together. He didn't even pause for a breath before saying, "Well, okay. I guess we will just get divorced. My uncle is a lawyer. I will set it all up." There was no discussion, no argument, no thought. It just happened. A week later, he had found me a place to live and moved me there, gave me five hundred dollars and the microwave, and that was that. Two years married, and two weeks divorced.

To say I was shell-shocked would be an understatement. In retrospect, our marriage never stood a chance, but at the time, I was devastated. My sense of slightly improving self-worth was torpedoed. This pivotal man said one thing to me that was the catalyst for a whole new direction in my life: "You will never be anything but an airman in your sad little air force life." I remember thinking I would show him what I could become. I now believe God provides the necessary crises to get us to wake up to our potentials if we aren't taking steps to do so on our own.

I want to add a short story that reminds me even in our darkest hour, we are not alone, and we are loved. I went to a small church shortly after my divorce rocked my world. In front of me, all I saw were couples and families. The view behind me was pretty much the same. To my left, at the other end of the pew, was a woman with a severely twisted spine and her little boy. The woman's condition made it hard for her to walk. At one point in the service, the congregation sang the Lord's Prayer, and everyone held hands.

I was too far away from the boy to hold his hand, and everyone else was a couple. I didn't even sing. I couldn't because I was so miserable and emotional. I just stood there, feeling sorry for myself and all alone.

A moment or so later, I felt a small hand in mine. The little boy had dragged his mother over, so he would be close enough to hold my hand. God looked down on me in that moment of sadness and through a small child, reminded me I was most definitely not alone. In great humility, he also showed me I have a responsibility to see the opportunities around me. I could have walked with ease to the boy and his mother.

What I now know is that my employment and leadership record is actually a record of my efforts to be liked, worthy, and accepted. Leadership gave me a vehicle to feel important and necessary. I do not regret any of these positions because I grew so much and began to see my worth through them. I realize that in each position, as well as in my first marriage, I was still looking through the lens of what someone else thought of me. I still hadn't figured out that it is what *I* think of my worth and value that matters. My fledgling military career, along with my rather brief first marriage, highlighted that I had a few more lessons to learn.

Questions to Ponder

What jobs or projects have you taken to impress or win the love of another?

_____

_____

_____

_____

_____

Did you find fulfillment in the jobs that you identified?

_____

_____

_____

_____

_____

Can you look at these events from a new perspective today and be grateful for the lessons that you learned?

_____

_____

_____

_____

_____

What are some of the lessons you learned through these experiences? List some of them here. Find a place of gratitude in your heart for those lessons and the circumstances that brought them to light. Gratitude is a key component to a positive perspective and the release of judgment and disappointment.

_____

_____

_____

_____

_____

CHAPTER 5

A New Direction

I decided to go to school. After all, that was why I joined the military. I went to night and weekend classes through the Emery Riddle University Military Extension program. I still worked full time and strove toward enlisted promotions while I worked on my university degree. The first thing I will say about this is that this path toward a degree is not easy. I pretty much had no time for anything extra. In one sense, it was good, though, because I was still reeling from my marriage imploding in one quick blast.

The second thing I will say is that I got straight As. Wait a minute! I thought I wasn't smart. I was twenty-five and still firmly believed I was lousy at school. At first, I thought maybe the instructors were just kind. But after a while, I began seriously enjoying the classes and learning everything— except for algebra. I was terrorized throughout algebra because, well … it was math! I cried all during the final exam for fear I would fail. I didn't, however, but received my first and only B of my degree program. I was ecstatic!

As crazy as it sounds, this newly found intelligence was such an odd concept to me. I spent a lifetime believing I was stuck in the remedial lane. Here I was, taking classes, loving learning, and rocking a grade point. Discovering my new status as a smart person was when I truly started to question some of my negative and limiting beliefs. Most of my teachers were air force officers who held master's degrees and moonlighted as professors. They were all so encouraging, especially because they recognized working all day and going to school at night was a tough row to hoe.

The officers I provided administrative support for became my family, coming to my important events and encouraging me. They planted a bug in my ear that when I graduated, I should apply for the officer training course (OTS). I had forgotten the vow I made to my former husband to become an officer after earning a degree. My choice to apply for this training was no longer about him. It was all about me, which was a nice change of pace.

Throughout my university/work journey, I had many helpers and pseudo-family members. A very special family stand-in was—is—Phyllis, a counselor I started seeing after my husband abruptly left me. She has a heart of gold, serious clarity, and a ready laugh. I often think it was our ability to laugh that saved me. I saw her for about two years professionally, until such time we agreed that we could move from the counselor-counselee stage to true friendship.

I became like a sister and aunt to her kids, and to this day, I call her my proxy mom. Her youngest and I are kindred spirits. This counselor came to every graduation, awards ceremony, and anything else that I wanted or needed her to attend. My father was on his own tangent to get married and live his life, which meant he didn't have time to come see me. My mom would have liked to attend but didn't have the money. Nor did I, so she missed all my events.

I eventually, graduated in the top 2 percent of my class. I was truly amazed and felt exceptionally good. I even had a nice boyfriend. I applied for OTS and was accepted. My boyfriend, an enlisted man, declared that I needed to decide between love and promotion. Thank goodness for my officer family and Phyllis! They gave me the courage to recognize this was another form of manipulation, and I was better and more deserving than that. I chose OTS. Sorry, boyfriend!

OTS sent me back to Texas, where I originally took basic training. I drove around the town near the base for hours, trying to work up the nerve to go back to basic training! That old fear of not being worthy was trying mightily to get me to turn around and head home. But I didn't give in. Far too many people had encouraged me. I think it was the fear of facing them in defeat that finally got me to drive on to the base and confront whatever I found.

What I eventually learned was that OTS is nothing like basic training. It is a leadership laboratory. It is twelve weeks long and broken into two sections. In the first section, I was in the lowerclassmen category. The people in the second section were now upperclassmen and responsible for the lowerclassmen. The course is designed like a military base, with squadrons, commands, flights, and people in charge of each of those areas. There were also support and operations officers. Each student had a real officer to help guide him or her.

This structure is actually brilliant. Rather than yelling like in enlisted basic training, we received a different kind of pressure. We were given too much to do and observed, graded, and awarded on how we prioritized and helped each other. I never went off base on weekends because I chose to ignore the ever-present dust bunnies under my bed and focus on my schoolwork. For those of you who have never looked under your bed, a dust bunny is that ball of fuzz made up of hair, dust, and particles that magically appear out of nowhere. If one doesn't sweep the floor regularly, they multiply like bunnies—thus, dust bunnies! I got busted for a dirty room all the time. Damn dust bunnies! By the way, you really ought to look under your bed every so often. It might be weirder than you think. Whole cultures might have formed in your absence.

Toward the end of the first six weeks, we applied or were

nominated for positions of leadership for our second half of training. My real officer, Captain B, wanted me to apply for OTS commander. That is the position over all other students. He said he recognized natural leadership in me, that I was intelligent (wow), and had a way of supporting people that made getting the job done a given. I must admit, I felt about ten feet tall. It also scared the crap out of me. I know now that true growth comes when we step outside our comfort zones.

This application put me way outside my comfort zone. But I did it anyway and won the position. For six weeks, I was going to be the OTS commander over four hundred people. Yikes!

That time was some of the hardest and included some of the most enjoyable moments of my military career. The pressure on all of us was intense, and as I mentioned during my basic training phase, this was intended to determine if we would break under pressure. Some did. My flight (about twenty people) lost a young man who literally snapped one day. He became almost catatonic. Then he became violent. Fortunately, there were already paramedics on the scene, and he received the help he needed. He was supposed to be a pilot too. Thank goodness they found out he was mentally unstable before he got into a flying weapon.

The graduation parade and swearing in came at the end of OTS. Graduation day was an amazing one for me because it was one event in my life that my father attended. He was so proud of me becoming an officer. He had the honor of swearing me in as he was a retired officer. The picture of us during the swearing in shows him with a huge, puffed chest and a raised right hand. He could not have been taller that day, and I was glad to see him like that. I am pictured standing opposite him. Admittedly, what I still see when I look at that picture is my potbelly. Clearly, I still need to work on this self-image thing!

Then came the parade. There were reviewing stands (bleachers) down one side of the parade field, which was about the size of a football field. In the center of the row of bleachers was

a covered stand where all the VIPs and generals sat. My father was
seated in the bleacher section to their left. The parade consisted
of myself in the front and two of my staff, one on each side of
and slightly behind me. We three were in front of the crowd of
graduating airmen and lowerclassmen. That meant four hundred
people, broken into four squadrons or units, marched behind me.

Nobody moved until the music started, and I gave the
command. It was pretty heady, I have to admit, and nerve-
racking. What if I started on the wrong foot? When the music
started, I called out, and the long train of people began to move.
We went all around the right side of the field, so we would end
up passing in front of the general's stand at the very end, passing
my father in the process. My two colleagues were giving me a
hard time the whole way, teasing me that I was going to mess up
the call to salute.

What they didn't know was that I intended to call the salute
just a moment or so early, so I could salute my father. Although
startled when I called, "Eyes right," early, their training kicked
in, allowing them to react accordingly, and my dad received a
very long salute! I was thrilled because he knew what I had done.

After the parade, we went to the officer's dining hall for lunch
because we could; I was now an officer. This day provided me one
of my favorite memories of my dad. For that day, there was no
other thing except his pride in his daughter. It was pretty much
the only time I ever felt it. We grew a bit closer because of the tie
I now had with him as a military officer. I think this started my
trajectory to finding true self-confidence as well.

I went to Davis Monthon Air Force Base in Arizona for my
first assignment as an officer. I was blessed to have a tough but
fair boss, a female full colonel. She taught me what it meant to be a
leader in so many different ways. You see, while I was in Arizona,
Saddam Hussein attacked Kuwait, and America responded. I
found myself on a plane headed to the United Arab Emeritus with

ninety other people from our base. Many were going to work for me, providing logistical support to a base.

The goal was to meet up with a commander and his troops from another base and form one big unit. That commander had been a hostage in Iran for over a year, and when he received orders to deploy to the area again, he refused. He said he had already served, and the air force agreed. They failed to send a replacement, however, so I landed at two in the morning on a very hot, muggy night with frightened people only to find out I was to be the commander. There was no going back or complaining. I knew if we were going to succeed, I had to put my fears and insecurities in my duffle bag and step up to the plate.

I was there for seven months as a second lieutenant, the lowest rank for an officer. I was a logistics commander with sixty plus people under me in a war zone. My peers were all several ranks ahead of me. To add interest to this scenario, my stateside real commander deployed as the logistics commander at the base a few miles down the road. Now my boss became my peer as I was the logistics commander at the base near Abu Dhabi. I was incredibly fortunate because she treated me like a commander but still provided counsel if needed. It was an amazing experience.

The seven months I was in Desert Shield/Desert Storm (the operational name for this engagement), I grew in so many ways. I became a very good leader, who was fortunate to have terrific people working for me. They made the long days bearable. I was even put in for a Bronze Star, although someone in a high place determined I was not high enough in rank to earn that medal. Don't worry; I was decorated nicely for this service. The Bronze Star would have been nice as my grandfather earned one in World War II, and I would have been able to use his medal in the ceremony. Oh well. I know what I accomplished there and am proud to say I did a damn good job, thank you very much. What's more, I did it as a second lieutenant!

There were a few defining moments in the seven months that

I would like to share. Leadership can certainly be exhilarating, but it can also be terribly lonely. I was well liked but not part of the crowd. My rank kept me apart from the people I commanded, and I was too junior in rank to hang out with the officers with whom I served. There were certainly people I could trust. In particular was one of my airmen who always worked nights.

His name was KP, and I could always find him around two or three in the morning, when I was working nights or couldn't sleep and needed to blow off steam. He would ask me, "LT, you need to talk?" Then he and I would sit on the tarmac and just talk about nothing in particular. He was the sounding board I needed. For me, he was an angel in human form and helped me survive a tough assignment. But he was not the only angel to visit me.

Christmas was right around the corner, and America was determined to remember the soldiers overseas. In late October, we started to receive any servicemen packages. We found boxes filled with toiletries, games, and movies; we had a little tent-side theater with a TV and video machine in the center of the came. All sorts of things were sent to us. Each squadron got a stack of these boxes when they came in, and I always ensured that my folks got them all. I didn't feel right taking one when there were people below me who I thought should receive them. One day toward Christmas, I was having a bit of an internal pity party. I had not received any cards, boxes, or any indication I had a family back in the States. It shouldn't have surprised me given that no one in my family is good at sending cards. I felt quite alone.

One of my troops asked to come into my office tent. He gave me a box about the size of a shoebox. He said he thought I ought to have at least one gift, so he picked one out of the latest shipment and brought it to me. I thanked him and set the box aside. Later, when I was alone, I opened the box. It held an angel made from a plastic grid and yarn. It was most likely a simple kit for beginning crafters.

The angel stands about ten inches high and has a little set

of wings I can slide in the back of the angel body. The face has no features; it is a round ball with yarn hair. There was a note that simply said, "You are not alone." I used the present tense to describe this angel because, twenty-five years after this experience, it is still one of my most treasured gifts. When I opened that box, I believe God reminded me yet again that I was most definitely not alone.

My military career took me to several places before eventually leading to Norway, where I started working for the North Atlantic Treaty Organization (NATO). And where I met my future husband, whom I will refer to only as "my husband" to protect his privacy. We moved to Italy after we got married. We lived in Naples, a wonderful, chaotic, beautiful, dirty city. It was in Naples that my spiritual transformation started. It all started with a pull on my heart to do something more. To be something more than the roles I currently played. I answered the pull and explored all sorts of avenues for personal growth. The concept of my own identity was forced to change through different courses of study and life events that shook my marriage.

Questions to Ponder

Have specific events caused you to change your life direction?
What were some of them?

_____

_____

_____

_____

_____

In retrospect, did the new direction turn out to be beneficial for
you? How?

_____

_____

_____

_____

_____

Have you been surprised by an unexpected angel? How?

_____

_____

_____

_____

_____

CHAPTER 6

Spiritual Paths Are Relentless

Spiritual paths are relentless. What I mean by "spiritual path" is the course of self-study that looks at what drives or limits our lives. It is the deep questioning of everything within and outside our personal worlds. Once one starts down this internal path, there is no going back. Remember the popular *Matrix* movie? The hero is offered a blue pill that will allow him to continue living in a dream. Or he can take the red pill and wake up to the true nature of reality.

Here is the rub, however. Once you take the red pill, you can't take the blue pill after and forget what you have seen after taking the red pill. It is one or the other. A spiritual path is like that. Once you decide to dig deeper into what makes you who you are and what are the driving forces in the universe, an awareness awakens that cannot be turned off. I truly believe the spiritual path is the first step toward finding inner happiness, which reflects as outer beauty.

I grew up in a normal, middle-American Christian home. We had our share of dysfunction, but nothing too terrible. I certainly didn't suffer or go hungry. Like most parents, mine did the best they could with the information they had. They sought to teach us right from wrong, the basics of money, and how to be a responsible

47

person in an often irresponsible world. And, of course, they taught us about God, at least from their understanding.

My family went to a conservative Lutheran church with the requisite Sunday school. I made it my mission to memorize as much as I could so I could shine. Many of the lessons I memorized stay with me today. My view of God has changed, but the concepts I internalized remain. I know I am loved and that I am not alone. I also know we are meant to be kind to each other and love everyone. As adults, this sometimes becomes much easier said than done. I don't remember many of the verses from so long ago. Concepts yes ... verses, not so much. Where does the memory go as we get older?

I liked church well enough as a child. There were always lots of people, and I enjoyed singing. Somewhere along the journey, I learned God was somewhere out there, and I was very far away from him. The standard image of the man looking like the wizard Gandalf with a flowing white beard took hold in my mind at that time. Okay, God was never actually imagined in this way, but there was a definite suggestion that he was very separate from the rest of us. I understood that God was definitely out there, watching. Spiritual fear was born. Unless I got it right, I would go to hell, which is an awfully long way away from the Gandalf God I imagined.

At some point, the Lutheran church structure split due to church politics at its finest from what I heard. I didn't understand much except that we ended up switching churches. We went to a Pentecostal church for a while. It was decidedly livelier than the Lutheran church. There were a lot of hands in the air and speaking in tongues. I understood that speaking in tongues was allowing the spirit to move through you in prayer, but I didn't like it; mostly because I couldn't do it. I don't remember anything else about this church. I believe however, my earliest concepts of the Universal Spirit came from this church. It always is fascinating to me what I discover when I reflect on events in my life.

Fast-forward many years to Naples, Italy. At the base where I was stationed, I started taking yoga. My instructor was the epitome of beauty and spirituality. I hung on her every word. I probably put her on a bit of a pedestal, and in retrospect, I don't think she minded that very much. I wanted to be like her, teach yoga, and embrace all the new (to me) Eastern philosophies.

My husband was gracious and supported me taking lessons and even traveling for a month at Christmas to Austria to go to yoga school. He was not particularly interested in discussing the wholeness of life or the spirit that moves us all. He was an engineer, and unless there was a model to put a concept in, he could not wrap his head around it. I was disappointed because I hoped he would share my interest, but he didn't. And, of course, I understood. This habitual understanding was my fallback position for any interaction. He supported me, and that was something I appreciated.

My yoga instructor and her husband were also students of crop formations. You may have heard of crop circles or formations. One year they invited me to England to see some of these formations, and I went with enthusiasm. These formations are truly a mystery. No one knows how they are made or who makes them. The earliest formations documented were in 1678, so they are hardly new. They are extraordinarily beautiful though. As a quilter—quilting is one of my hobbies—I was intrigued by the patterns and designs. As an individual, I was blown away by the size, complexity, and sheer beauty of these crop formations. If you want to know more, go to www.cropcircleconnector.com.

Several things happened on my first trip to see the crop formations. First, I felt the energy of the formations. People enter them and feel differently. Some say it is a vibration or resonance. Whatever it is, I felt it. I became aware that there was more to my physical world than I understood, and I wanted to know more. I also learned about dousing with copper rods and using a pendulum to detect energy shifts. I was completely hooked.

Let me just say something about using tools to detect energy. They are not the devil's tools or work. All dousing or divining methods are centuries old. They use the energy all around us to show what we are looking for. When we are open to our energy, we can quite literally tap into the energy all around us and detect changes in the energy patterns. For me, this was very cool, and I wanted to know more.

I was also introduced to a woman who channeled angels. I have always believed that we have a celestial support team who helps us all. There are just too many seeming coincidences and circumstances in our lives not to think we don't get an occasional nudge in a different direction. Some people can step away from their egos and relax into the information all around us. Some tap into specific energy known as channeling. This woman's name is BJ, and she relaxes into the energy of specific angels helping specific individuals. I was intrigued because I had so many questions. The idea of getting answers was delicious. I was also open-minded enough to explore this option.

I was still living in Italy, and this woman I had never met was in Virginia. We met over the phone one night. My husband was listening because he suspected she was nothing more than a creative trickster. He trusted me so was open to at least entertaining the idea. BJ suggested I relax and mentally invite my angels to join me. She was quiet and getting herself out of the way, as she described it.

When she said she was ready, I thought her voice would change or some other interesting thing might happen. It did not. The person on the other end of the phone sounded just as she had two minutes before. What she had to say, however, was relatively profound for me. I started by asking the angels if they had anything to say to me. They told me I was at the beginning of a great awakening. That my heart was opening, and the brightness of it was beautiful; it was like looking in awe at a field of poppies. I felt loved. I always loved poppies, so that was cool too.

The next hour was full of questions and answers. There were several things said about me that no one knew or that BJ could not have known as she didn't know me. I left the phone call more curious than before. I knew I would not stop seeking more knowledge about the world around me. But my husband was confused. The idea of channeled messages definitely didn't fit a model he knew, and that frightened him. Sadly, I think this was the beginning of the end for us because the more open I became, it appeared the more afraid he became and, in some ways, more rigid in his beliefs.

I understood his discomfort. I wish it were different, but I truly get that each of us has our own path to follow, and sometimes they go in different directions. One is not better than the other; they are just different.

I met with BJ telephonically every few months as I learned more about my spiritual side. My angels suggested I could use my compassion and healing touch to help others heal. I thought I was way too old to go to medical school. I felt the same about becoming a nurse. I had no idea what becoming a healer might look like in my life.

One day at the gym, a woman I barely knew said she was starting an energy-healing group and asked if I wanted to join. I will call her Dee. She was the wife of a British officer I knew and respected; they went to our church. While surprised, I jumped at the opportunity. My husband had less difficulty with this, perhaps because he was well acquainted with the officer and thought if it was okay with him, there was nothing to worry about. Dee encouraged several other church women to join the healing group too. Including people we knew made the concept of an energy-healing group less scary for all, especially my husband.

There are a variety of energy-healing styles. Some styles are more common, like reiki and therapeutic touch. Others are less so, like the healing modality called LaHo-Chi, which is what we practiced in this group. What all energy-healing modalities have, however, is the intention of love and service to the person who is hurting or in need. When we approach another like a mother would a wounded child, with our hearts open and in compassion, we literally radiate healing energy. The receiver feels warm, relaxed, and peaceful. In that state, the body will be in a perfect place to start healing itself.

Our bodies are amazing. They constantly make minor adjustments and repairs. It happens so seamlessly that we frequently don't even know it is happening. When we are deeply stressed or have sustained a serious injury or illness, our bodies are still designed to heal. However, at that point, we are usually so stressed that we inhibit the body from healing. Energy healers help a person enter a state of deep relaxation that lets the body return to its natural mission of rejuvenation.

Today, many major hospitals use energy-healing modalities. In fact, for several years, I volunteered at the Flagstaff Cancer Center, giving reiki to patients before they went for chemo. The American Cancer Society endorses reiki and other energy-healing modalities as additional beneficial treatments to chemo. Science has come so far in being able to measure the energetic field around all things. It is now understood that all things in life, include non-living things, are made of energy in movement. We have only touched the tip of the energetic iceberg!

One of the great lessons I learned in my early stages of energy work is that it is not up to me to determine how healing unfolds. When doing energy-healing work, there is sometimes quite a strong sensation, like a swirling or movement even though I stood still for the most part. While I moved around the person on the table, I often felt either heat, a tingling sensation, or a swirling sensation in my hands.

Sometimes the person receiving felt it, and sometimes they didn't. When working with other people, it always fascinated me that when one of us felt the need to move, all of us did. We did not coordinate our movements. We usually had our eyes closed, but we all felt the need to move at the same time, as if it were planned. I never bumped into another healer. It was what I referred to as an energetic dance.

These sensations and feelings could be a bit addictive. Each time I worked with someone, I wanted to experience the feeling again. That, of course, was when I realized I was focusing on myself, not the one I was supposed to be serving. Some people healed by releasing fears, even though the physical symptoms remained the same. Some healed by a peaceful death without any fear. Some healed by actual physical healing. Admittedly, I especially liked it when that happened. I had to remind myself that I was merely the instrument of the energy, not the actual cause of healing.

I loved the healing work and the time I spent with this amazing group of women and a few men. Each one made it his or her mission to help others in need and teach others their own abilities in healing touch. At the same time, my personal life was taking a turn for the worse. I will not go into detail, but two things particularly were the driving factors toward this decline in marital bliss. The first was that we were not nurturing our marriage. We supported each other very well, but that is very different from nurturing a marriage. We spent all our time helping other family members through sickness and their marital problems while putting no focus on our marriage.

The second factor was something that I previously mentioned. The more open I became to the wonders of the unseen universe, the more close-minded or, dare I say, fearful my husband seemed to become. He still supported my desire to learn and take classes. I even went on week-long classes in the States. I tried to help him understand, which conceptually he did. He just wasn't sure what to do with the information. I was not particularly helpful in that regard, mostly because I didn't know what I was trying to accomplish with all my studies and learning. The fact of the matter was that what excited me just wasn't in his desired realm of understanding.

I found myself in the uncomfortable position of knowing I could not continue living a double life. My husband and I were growing farther apart. We each supported the other's hobbies but did not participate in any together. One year, I went to a women's yoga retreat in California. Our plan was for my husband to join me in Arizona afterward for a much-needed vacation.

One evening at the retreat there was a sing-along with all of us raising our voices and dancing. After a short time, I noticed I was dancing by myself away from the other participants. What struck me about this situation was that it was an apt metaphor for how I was living. I was dancing by myself through my marriage, work, and even some friendships. At that moment, with all these women all around me, I felt alone. I realized I was holding myself back from participating in the wellspring of universal love that was pulling me toward a different path, and I was too busy trying to keep the status quo alive.

Many more thoughts raced through my brain. But at that moment, I knew it was time to leave everything and start over. I had taken the red pill a few years before, and there was no going back. My spirit longed to follow my dreams. My husband, whom I cared for deeply but knew I was no longer in love with— nor he with me, was holding me back. The status quo was no longer okay. I left the retreat with the courage to leave the man I cared so deeply for and forge a new life. I had no idea what that would look like. I just knew I didn't have a choice.

Some of the shifts we make when we choose to follow our hearts and intuitions can be frightening. They can upset a very well-established applecart. It took great courage to follow the heart and do what I knew needed to be done for me to grow and embrace all my potential. I had no idea what the future would hold, but for the first time in my life, I focused on what was right for me. I felt selfish because this was a new feeling. I had spent a lifetime focusing on others, pleasing others, doing what others expected. Focusing on myself for once felt good.

I approached leaving with great compassion toward my husband. But if I am to be truly transparent, I was ecstatic that for once, I was chasing my happiness by and through my own actions. It was very liberating right, alongside slightly terrifying. Looking back to that time now, I have no regrets. I took my desire to be loved and flipped it into an internal love. Tentative at first, with the real knowledge that I was just beginning to become. "Become what?" you ask. I didn't really know at the time. And that was part of the beauty of the entire experience.

Questions to Ponder

Do you consider yourself on a spiritual path? (inward exploration)

_____

_____

_____

_____

_____

What callings have you experienced?

_____

_____

_____

_____

_____

How did you get past the discomfort and forge forward with courage?

_____

_____

_____

_____

_____

What do you need to heal in your life? Is it physical, emotional, spiritual, or a blend of all three?

_____

_____

_____

_____

CHAPTER 7

Jack-of-All-Trades, Master of None, Lessons in All

As I look back on the many jobs and opportunities I have had, I realize that I've lived what most would consider a terrific life. I traveled around the world, performed a variety of interesting jobs, lived on four continents, and have never been hungry once. Additionally, I have never known what I wanted to be or do; nor did I ever feel particularly confident in what I was doing. I find myself in real admiration of people who have the drive to be or do something specific, like be an athlete or entrepreneur. To see the focus it takes to be an ironman or world-class ice-skater is something to behold. Where does that drive come from, and how did these people determine what they wanted to be or do?

I can remember thinking so many times that I wanted to become something or accomplish something great. I had idea after idea and pursued many of them. While I had some success at almost everything I tried, I never settled into anything specific. I always felt a yearning for something different. The result is that I became a jack of multiple trades and a master at none of them. Don't misunderstand me. I am not putting myself down because as I noted before, I was pretty much successful at everything I have done. I have won awards, earned degrees, earned promotions, and the like. However, I have always moved on to something new. A friend once said that I was like Madonna in that I reinvent myself every few years. Clearly, I have great friends!

As I have grown older, I've become a bit more reflective and, as such, have tried to understand my mixed bag of careers and wandering mind. Is there a theme from which I can glean some understanding? What do they all have in common? What are my memories of each of these careers? Good, bad, and in some cases, cringe moments.

What I know now is that all the moments, careers, and events of my life played a vital role in working through my limiting beliefs, self-doubt, self-disgust, and disappointment. Each stage of my life was necessary for me to grow into the wonderful person I am today. I sometimes wonder what my life would have been like if I had learned each necessary lesson on the first situational opportunity. Perhaps you find yourself making the same mistakes over and over and wondering why you keep repeating uncomfortable patterns.

Good spot to throw in a helpful quote.

> Life will give you whatever experience is most helpful for evolving your consciousness. How do you know that this is the experience that you need? Because this is the experience that you are having in the moment. (Eckhart Tolle)

You see, I believe the universe keeps giving us opportunities to grow and learn in all stages of our lives. If we don't get a lesson in one situation, life generously offers us another opportunity and another if needed until we learn the lesson and can move on. It is important to note that in the moment of the event meant to teach us; we often don't see what is going on.

Life is meant to learn through experience instead of just

through our head and book knowledge. That is the theory according to Kari, in case you are wondering. The result of this theory is that now I can look back on my long list of jobs and understand them much better. I can look at them now, release all judgment, and find gratitude for how they contributed to my growth and understanding of life.

When I first started working, I had a restaurant phase in high school and a few years after school. During those five or so years, I worked at seven restaurants. I was a server at times and an assistant manager at others. I was becoming an adult with a serious lack of self-worth. Restaurants put me smack-dab in the middle of a lot of people—customers, coworkers, bosses, and lovers. I didn't think I was very pretty and everyone else was prettier and smarter than me. This made me a prime target for hormonal men. I also wanted to be part of the crowd, and the newly released from high-school masses were all about experimenting with everything. That combination was not great for my already poor self-image.

As I have grown to love myself through my spiritual journey, I had the hardest time with this phase. It wasn't pretty. My cringe moments involved waking up and not having a clue where I was or who I was with due to God knows what I consumed the night before. I even had one stint with a man who turned out was married and way over possessive to the point of guns and scary standoffs! Thank goodness for police and a family I discovered loved me no matter what, regardless of what I previously thought. As a matter of fact, it was that scary incident that opened my eyes to the fact that not only was I loved by my family but fiercely so!

My younger years didn't see this demonstrated very well. But this incident made their love quite clear. What I learned in those years was powerful because I came to understand that I am a good leader, an excellent teacher, and can rise above my embarrassment no matter what and move on. I no longer cringe at the memories of that time. In fact, through deep compassion for and forgiveness of myself, I now know this was a time of tremendous growth for me. It was a time when I decided to at least respect my body, even though I hadn't quite arrived at the point of liking it.

My military phase involved multiple jobs. ATC was not for me. I learned that getting a job to please another person was not the right thing for me. I was so afraid to tell my father I was leaving ATC because I just knew he would be disappointed. His reaction startled me because it was very supportive. Maybe he had grown too. Leaving that job for an administrative position helped put a little crack in the limiting belief that my dad expected me to follow in his footsteps in avionic jobs. What he wanted was for me to have a paying job that with opportunities, which the military can certainly provide.

The next few years of my military career were some of my biggest growth years. What I loved was that I was surrounded by people who needed me. I was gaining confidence, and I had the attention of men interested in me for something other than a one-night stand. I arrived at a place where I demanded more for myself as well. In fact, I was respected and encouraged. My military family was special to me. My enlisted time was filled with some personal sadness due to my first divorce and some great growth due to my education and subsequent transition from enlisted person to officer.

At that transition, I became a logistics officer, which was great fun. Logistics personnel have their hands in everyone's business. It was a pretty good career that took me all over the world. I ended up in Norway, where I met my second husband. Did I mention he was Italian? Needless to say, my next destination was Italy, where I lived for fifteen years.

In Norway, I started quilting. I was going to be the best quilter in the world. I love the color and putting patterns together. Then I moved to Italy and got involved in a wonderful quilting group. Then I discovered I had only scratched the surface of quilting. I also discovered my status as world's best quilter was miles away! What impeded me more than anything was that I didn't actually like the quilting part, just the piecing. I still piece projects together quite successfully, but now I send them to master quilters to finish. This hobby goes into the enjoyment pile versus the I'm-going-to-make-a-living-pile. I even considered opening a craft store on a military base in Italy. That didn't work either. Another career choice came after I took up yoga, which I thoroughly enjoyed.

By this time, I was in my mid to late thirties with a pretty inflexible body. The lady who taught me was tall, beautiful, and could tie herself in a knot. I started to study yoga not just because I enjoyed it but because I wanted to be part of this amazing community of lithe, spiritual people. I can now see that much of what drove me was a desire to *be them* instead of a desire to be me. I even went to Thailand to take a two-week intensive course in yoga. The instructor was pompous, self-indulgent, and rude. He almost single-handedly turned me off yoga. My inner wisdom prevailed, however, and I continued my studies to the point of getting my teaching certificate. I began to see myself having a thriving business teaching yoga. My reality was slightly different but still enjoyable.

I started teaching one class three times a week at my military base in Italy. I loved teaching. I can say without hesitation that I was good at it too. I longed for a teacher to work with, but my location made that difficult. The teacher I spoke of before had returned to the States with her husband. My teachers were from videos and books, which is not quite the same. I did get to take courses occasionally, which were helpful. While I never did develop an amazing yoga following, this was a time of great spiritual growth for me.

I started studying all manner of metaphysical things, including angels, crop circles, quantum energy, and meditation. Remember my teacher's comment that the journey is the focus? I still think that comment would make a dandy title for a book.

Well, twenty years later, I am finally writing my book. However, like my life, the focus of this book changed to reflect what I now feel is my true mission. Now I know my true purpose is helping people, particularly women, lose their limiting beliefs about themselves so they may embrace their beauty and power.

After I returned to the United States, having left pretty much everything behind, I intended to open a healing arts studio for the practice of yoga, energy healing, and teaching. I was convinced this was the next step in my evolution. After all, I had been a successful member of an energy-healing group, I taught yoga to a faithful following of NATO employees and spouses, and I taught people new to the energy-healing world how to tap into their healing powers. I moved to Flagstaff, Arizona. At that time, I didn't have to work for the near foreseeable future and could focus on my studio. I worked on following my intuition. I had just one small problem. I still didn't believe in myself. This did not bode well for my progress.

After moving to Flagstaff, I attended different yoga classes to get a feel for the teachers. They were all so good. I thought, *I better wait to start my classes rather than tap into a thriving community. I don't want them to see that I am not a master.* I got caught up in comparing myself to people with completely different styles rather than let my natural teaching ability carry me.

I was even caught in a subtle trap of thinking if I looked the part, maybe I would have more credibility. I don't even want to tell you how many cute yoga outfits I have! I now know that great yoga pants do not a yogi make. What held me back from so much opportunity was my doubt. I doubted my ability, my looks, and my gifts. I see that now, but then I was wearing habitual negative blinders to my potential. I thought, *Surely opportunity will present itself and boom, I will be successful.* I was following my intuition after all, and that had to count for something.

I started a healing group people enjoyed. But everyone moved away, and it fizzled. I took class after class in Sedona, an energy mecca if you will. Then I had the opportunity to set up shop in a doctor's office with a doctor and her companion, a nurse practitioner. Aha! I had finally arrived at the door of my healing center. There was just one problem. After I set up my room in their suite of offices, the doctor and nurse practitioner made an executive decision.

They didn't want to give the practice a too esoteric vibe, so they wanted me to concentrate on their weight-loss program with clients for the first year. Then, if it felt right, I could start doing energy work. Being a weight-loss clinician was not what I signed up for, and in pretty short order, that plan disintegrated. I was discouraged and eventually went to work first as an office manager and then for a retailer. I picked up my old habitual patterns of seeking my worth by becoming a supervisor or a manager as I was so good with people, and I needed them to be good to me.

I plugged along in retail for a few more years. My sister, her daughter, and my mother moved from Philadelphia to join me in Flagstaff. At the time, due to some medical issues, all of them needed help that took a great deal of our time and energy. I now believe I was needed more for my family than the world at large, so the universe delayed my plans for a healing center. I couldn't see this then and struggled with a sense of loss and misdirection. Now I am grateful because I can see with a clearer heart that supporting my family in those few years was invaluable. Their support of me was equally so. The universe will always guide us where we need to be not just for ourselves but in service to others. If we pay attention—which most of us don't—we will see this beautiful pattern unfolding throughout our lives.

I entered a time of transition from disappointment about my unsuccessful goal achievement to truly see the wonder of what each part of my life allowed me to learn. I began to understand all the disconnected pieces of my life and careers were necessary puzzle pieces that, when put together, created the beautiful picture of who I am today. I began to shift my perspective from frustration to curiosity again, and this shift made all the difference for me going forward. Such a shift is vital if we are to truly grow.

By looking for opportunity instead of wading in disappointment, we can approach all of life's ups and downs from a new, more-empowering perspective. This new understanding is the part where the lessons become our silver lining on the clouds in our lives.

I am a real estate agent as well as a personal transformation coach. I have had a few speaking engagements, including a TEDx® talk given in Coeur d'Alene, Idaho. Now it looks like I can add author to the list. This year at least, I say with a smile. When I chose to go into real estate, a friend asked me how many jobs I have had, which set me to counting. Frankly, I lost count. I recently watched a TEDx® talk given in Bend, Oregon, by Emilie Wapnick. She discussed how some of us don't have one true calling. In it, she talked about people whose sense of purpose took them in multiple directions. Her talk is about why this is a good thing.

Emily coined the phrase *multipotentialite* to describe people who have so many ideas and passions. That seems like a good description for me. My early reasons for my ever-changing job path revolved around trying to please others or overcome fears. I now consider myself blessed to have experienced so many pathways of learning. However, my history of personal and spiritual unrest and unhappiness shows I didn't always think so.

Thank goodness I finally figured out it was okay to try different jobs, projects, and careers. Each afforded me opportunities to learn something about myself. Each offered me chances to let go of limiting beliefs. Every one of them helped me become the me I am today! For that, I am truly grateful for each experience in my life.

Questions to Ponder

What events or situations happened in your life that you didn't understand at the time but now know were there to help you grow as a person?

_____

_____

_____

_____

_____

Can you find gratitude for the events of your life, even the difficult ones, by finding the lessons in them?

_____

_____

_____

_____

When you reflect on past events in your life, can you let go of judgment and find compassion for yourself? If needed, can you find forgiveness for yourself? This is the great pathway to healing.

_____

_____

_____

_____

_____

To view the TEDx Coeur d'Alene talk titled 'Teach Your Inner Critic A New Story', visit www.conquerlifecoaching.com.

_____

_____

_____

_____

_____

CHAPTER 8

Leadership and Personal Vulnerability

I served in leadership roles in most of my jobs. I believe the reason is twofold. First, I always felt I had to prove myself, so I worked harder than everyone else and was frequently promoted. The second reason is that I am a good leader, so I attained positions that highlighted this strength. For me, leadership is a means to reduce personal vulnerability. All the roles I played and positions I held taught me that.

While I enjoyed guiding and teaching people, I have come to discover that by taking on these roles, I effectively isolated myself from deep relationships. I used leadership as a shield to protect myself. That was a powerful epiphany for me. That eye-opener occurred during the story I am about to tell. However, to make sense, the story must come first.

Sometimes this journey I am on moves so fast that I get whiplash. My recent epiphany on leadership is one case in point. It started innocently enough. I got mad, and then my mind spiraled out of control; I was left reeling. At the time of my epiphany, I was the manager of a health food store. I enjoyed my job overall, but like all jobs, it had its challenges. Knowing everything there is to know is one of them.

One day I walked into the buyer's office to find my assistant manager teaching one of our buyers something about the computer system. What he was teaching was something I really should have known a long time ago but didn't. I got mad. I thought out loud and somewhat obnoxiously that I resented not having proper training. You see, my training had been somewhat lacking, and I had to make up for lost time by learning the job mostly on my own.

Moments after that initial irritation came the thought that with every single job I ever had, there were issues with my training. I immediately wondered, *Why do I draw the struggle to overcome a lack of training in every job?* Truly, in every job there was an issue with a trainer leaving early, being sick, or not having time to train me. Instead, I had to train myself most of the time. I then realized not only had I trained myself, I succeeded at each job quite nicely. There must be something to this.

Seconds passed, and the thought that popped into my mind next was, *Who and what am I trying to prove myself to?* This thought reflected a question of personal worthiness for me. The thing is that I succeed; in fact, I almost always become the leader or manager of every project or job. If everyone else believes in me, why don't I believe in myself? I was stunned to truly realize I wasn't trying to prove myself to others. I was trying to prove my worth to myself!

My mind segued to my role as a leader. I always enjoyed the role, but it is a lonely one. I get along with everyone, but they always stay at a respectful distance. It suddenly dawned on me that I wore leadership like a shield. It protects me from the vulnerability of closeness. Ouch.

That whole series of thoughts and revelations happened in about a five-minute span of time. I was at work, so I went to my office and wrote, with tears in my eyes, some very quick notes to explore later. In those few moments I knew I hit upon a monumental truth in my life, and it would change me. I didn't know how, but I knew it would.

I began to explore the concept of leadership as a shield. I thought about other shields I had like my weight, which has been like padding to life for me. I looked at other things that threw up barriers to closeness. I have been told more than once that I am intimidating to many because I am a strong woman coming from military leadership background and have traveled the world; many people have not.

The fact is that many women in leadership positions must be strong to survive. To be taken seriously, it is almost as if we must wear a masculine mask. I never thought I was intimidating, and I still don't. I think my background makes me more grounded and more interesting, but I suppose it is true that I carry myself with confidence that others might not share.

With this shield to vulnerability truth released from my psyche, I explored what I wanted because now I felt liberated like I never had before. I decided I was ready for partnership and collaboration rather than directing preverbal traffic. The idea of partnership is a hard one to explore because I wasn't just standing around waving my arms and supervising while in positions of leadership. I thought I was in partnership working alongside my employees, which in reality is not the same thing as a true partnership. My situation was more working hard alongside but over my employees. Definitely not the same thing as the connection of true partnerships.

I always felt I was in deep collaboration with the people I worked with to make our store a success. The difference was that now I felt ready to give up simply leading people. I wanted to work by their sides in a dance of work, laughter, love, and service. I had no idea what that would look like or how it would take place. But somehow, I knew that it would.

One thing I have figured out about the universe we live in

is that the energy I put out there will draw similar energy back to me. With that in mind, I focused on what I truly enjoyed about my store manager job and the joyful interaction with my employees and most customers. At the same time, I was also deciding and clarifying what I thought would be the perfect characteristics of my dream job. This was an interesting exercise as I had no idea what I wanted to do.

Well, that was not entirely true. I knew I wanted to be a partner in a creative environment. Still a career chameleon, I just had to narrow my focus and figure out what the next iteration would be. I knew ideally I would like to work four days a week instead of five. I knew I enjoyed laughter and an environment where laughter was encouraged. I knew I enjoyed my income (hey, nothing wrong with that). I also really enjoyed mentoring and teaching. Finally, I loved working with people. Retail is fun if you let it be, so it would not have surprised me if I stayed in this field, although I was open to anything.

Another interesting aspect of this process of self-discovery has been trying to put into words this wave of understanding that liberated me, especially in describing this process to my family. I live with my mother, sister, and niece. It is relevant to note that my promotion from assistant manager to store manager of a health food store required a move. My family had already followed me to Arizona from Pennsylvania. Then they moved again to follow me to Idaho. They did this to stay together and support each other.

At the time of my big epiphany, I had been in this job for only seven months. This revelation of liberation came pretty darn close on the heels of the move to Idaho. It was a long, expensive, and pretty exhausting move. Announcing that I didn't want to be a leader anymore would take a bit of delicate discussion.

You can only imagine my family's discomfort at hearing me talk about this idea, which would most likely involve another job change. As I explored this concept with them, I was met with a great deal of fear that I was going to walk off my job. That was the furthest thing from my mind, and I definitely didn't want to move again. I am convinced that we were all drawn to our current location for a reason. Even though it was a long move, everything about it fell into place with almost miraculous, albeit expensive, ease. There was some divine intervention to be sure.

I tried to assure them I was only exploring the whole revelation, not jumping off a cliff. After a while, I decided it was an exploration to make on my own as it was and is my journey. I didn't want to do anything make others uncomfortable, although this could happen anyway.

I continued working as a manager, although my soul called me to find something else. I racked my brain, trying to figure out what I was being called to do. The job notifications were all for ones in offices or cubicles. None of them felt right. I applied for many of them anyway to see if I could at least get something going. I was overqualified for most. Annoying to say the least as no one was willing to give me a chance. I prayed, meditated, and journaled. Sometimes following your intuition is a fearful and foggy process.

I know if you keep taking action steps in some direction, your inner spiritual guidance system will eventually course correct. The key is to start moving in some direction, so the navigation system starts to work. Our inner guidance systems are like your car navigator. You put a thought or desire in there like an address. For the navigator to give directions, however, you need to be moving. I just kept looking and applying for jobs. I should note that none of the ones I applied for remotely appealed to me.

After months of work and false starts, while I was cooking breakfast by myself, I swear I heard the words "real estate" either out loud or in my mind. I even looked around to see if someone was there. I immediately felt peaceful and went to work researching the possibilities. What I found out is the field gives a person a lot of freedom with his or her schedule, but it takes tremendous work and years to get started and gain a reputation that will draw in clients. The dropout rate is something like 85 percent! Hmmm, let's see, train myself … check! Work hard … check! Overcome great odds … check! Real estate sounded like my type of job. It also has the added benefit of working in partnership with so many other people that maybe I could even make friends!

My family thought I would be good at real estate, but they were concerned I would prematurely leave my current job. They strongly encouraged me to stay there for another year and save money. I reluctantly agreed as I thought they might be right.

Here is the thing about the flow of the universe. It is like water in quantity as it is rather unstoppable. We are asked to trust our hearts, take chances, and be uncomfortable because in that state, we are more open to receive and grow. I made it seven more months before circumstances at the store became untenable, and I had to leave. Fear be damned! It was time to try out new waters.

Real estate is an excellent job but one that takes years to master and start earning a good living—unless you have a huge sphere of people who trust you immediately with the biggest purchase they will ever make. I didn't. I had only been in town for around a year and a half, and all that time as a store manager of a brand-new store. I worked and slept that first year. There was no time for friendships. The first year of real estate was very hard but necessary for me to learn several lessons.

The first was trust. Trust in the universe/God. Trust in my family's support. And trust in my ability to succeed. That first year was all about letting go of fear. There were many a day that I thought, *Perhaps I should just become a waitress part-time to pay the bills.* I have great respect for waitresses, by the way, as I did the job myself for many years. In real estate, I persevered and began to earn a modest income.

It was also during this year that I became acquainted with The Miracle Morning movement based on the book I mentioned at the very beginning of this tale. You have probably heard that when the student is ready, the teacher will come. My teacher came in the form of that little book. The author, Hal Elrod, suggested we sign up on *The Miracle Morning* Facebook page. There I found a support system like no other. I could discuss my dreams, expose my fears, and explore options with people from all over the world. I could also uplift and support like-minded people, exploring their dreams. Within this community, I got the courage to keep exploring my path to my purpose. Incidentally, through this community I also got the impetus to write this book.

Questions to Ponder

Have you erected shields in your life that you are ready to get rid of to feel free and joyful?

_____

_____

_____

_____

_____

How do you face and overcome your fears?

_____

_____

_____

_____

_____

What moments do you recall that you consider turning points or aha moments?

_____

_____

_____

_____

_____

CHAPTER 9

What if I Let Go of the Fear I Am not Enough?

My new career path gave me plenty of opportunities to work hard and interact with people. I enjoyed it, although it was a real challenge to let go of the certainty of a steady paycheck. I also struggled with schedules. I have a fair amount of discipline, but I still struggled with motivating myself to create some semblance of a regular schedule. I could no longer rely on a standard fixed schedule found in traditional jobs. I found myself becoming lethargic when I was not focused on trying to find the next client and hopefully the next paycheck. I also really missed teaching and mentoring people.

The little book I mentioned earlier, *The Miracle Morning*, was a game changer, at least for me. I always knew that if I got up earlier in the morning, I would get so much more done. What the book did for me was give structure to my morning. The structure was backed up with a bit of empirical data and stories to show why each suggestion is valid and worth doing. The idea of this book is that if you capture your morning, you can capture your day. The book outlined a series of morning practices designed to help someone wake up on purpose to enhance self-development and prep the person to have a successful day.

The suggested practice is called Life S.A.V.E.R.S.—silence, affirmations, visualization, exercise, reading, scribing. Scribing is simply journaling or writing, but the J or W didn't work for the acronym. I won't go into more detail but suggest you read the book. It takes little time, but LIFE S.A.V.E.R.S. could make a huge difference in your life. I bring this up because it was through this practice that I tackled many fears and limiting beliefs, especially as I worked through a huge career transition I wasn't entirely convinced was right for me. A big limiting belief for me has always been about my worth and beauty. I used my morning practice to get to the bottom of those beliefs and lessen their impact on my daily activities.

As I made time to read each morning, I went through many books in my to-read stack. Did you realize that if you read ten pages a day, you can finish approximately eighteen books a year? I focused on books that would teach me, provide me strategies for success on both business and personal levels, and ones to uplift me during my continued journey of self-discovery. I also started listening to Audible books in my car. I am a Realtor ®, so I am in my car a lot. My vehicle became a mobile university.

Through reading these motivational and inspirational books, meditation, affirmations, and visualizations, I realized I was living the classic life of negative what-ifs? We all do this to some extent because for years, we have been encouraged to ask, "What is the worst thing that can happen in any given situation?" We ask, "What is broken?" We wonder about all the negative things that can transpire because of something we are about to do. It is such a negative approach. Yet it is so ingrained in us that many do not realize the quality of their focused direction. I certainly didn't, and it was affecting everything in my life.

Most of us have a running dialogue in our minds at all times. It never seems to shut up. I am sometimes startled when I pay attention to my mind. I will be in a meeting or on the phone and suddenly realize there is a song running through my mind. Or worse, a whole conversation happening. Usually some sort of rehearsal in preparation for the next time I get to speak. Or rehashing an event that didn't go the way I wanted. In reality, what is happening is that I am not fully present for whatever I am doing at the moment. This mental conversation is where the crazy roller-coaster ride of what-ifs takes place. Sometimes our mental rehearsing starts with something like, "If he says this, I will say that." It is almost like we are preparing for battle, using the word *if* as a sword!

What if this happened, or what if that happened? It is like a game that can spiral out of control when our minds jump on the habitually negative what-if bandwagon. I encourage you now to notice if your what-ifs tend to be negative.

What if they think I am ugly?

What if I am not enough?

What if he doesn't like me?

What if I don't get the job?

What if I lose the job I have?

What if I can't lose weight?

What if I fail?

What if the plane loses an engine? (I think any flyer has that on the mind even if for only a moment.)

What-if is frequently a game of fear. It percolates under the skin and in our psyches, holding us back, making us hesitate, and causing us stress. This game can keep us from really living if we let it. Sadly, many people let fear rule the day. Our limiting beliefs, which predicate the negative what-if question, blind us to the possibilities that surround us. We even limit our ability to think clearly when we are stuck in a cycle of negative questioning. I am not a scientist, but a lot of research shows that our neurotransmitters do not function well in a negative state. They don't light up with possibility. It takes courage to change the course of our questioning to a more positive, strength-based path. But it can be done, and the benefits are completely worth it.

Courage in hand, let's explore the other side of the what-if game, the positive side; the sunny side of life if you will. It is a shift in perspective that, with practice, can become a habit. I promise this shift will change you for the better. More important, an appreciative what-if is liberating and full of possibilities. Dr. Barbara Fredrickson, a leading researcher in the field of positive psychology, demonstrated that when we are in a positive frame of mind, our neurotransmitters light up with possibilities. We become more creative.

What if they think I look wonderful? An even better choice to start with is, what if *I* think I look wonderful?

What if I am exactly right for the role I want to play?

What if he does like me?

What if I get the job?

What if I keep the job that I currently have or maybe get a promotion?

What if I become healthy and trim?

What if the plane works like a champ? (That, of course, is what we all want!)

For me, the positive what-ifs were just as scary and limiting as the negative ones. When one struggles with a weak sense of self-worth or worthiness, there is an underlying fear of success that can be debilitating. You might be thinking that fearing success doesn't make sense. Doesn't everyone want to be successful? Wouldn't life be so much easier if I were successful? The fact of the matter is that to fully enjoy success, you must believe you deserve it.

It was not until I learned to finally love myself and appreciate the essence of who I am that I could begin to not only attract more success but truly enjoy it as well. I experienced so much success in my various careers, but I was constantly afraid someone would figure out I was a fraud. Surely I had achieved the promotion or award because of the actions of others. I didn't enjoy my success because I didn't feel worthy of it.

For me, success turned out to be more about helping others succeed than any objective or achievement I might have reached. I suspect this was what made me such a good leader. My natural tendency to uplift and support others made for a successful work environment. With each success, I grew in my self-confidence, which eventually helped me overcome my irrational fear around worthiness of success.

The baseline of the what-if game is fear of not being enough and/or not being loved. These are our most primal fears, and if we let them, they will steer our lives in limited directions. These two base fears rob us of our light and beauty. They diminish our possibilities and steal our freedom. Negative fears and limiting beliefs affect us all to varying degrees.

These fears are the result of our early childhood and societal programming, as well as the never-ending onslaught of advertisements that make us feel less than [fill in the blank]. These base fears are enhanced because most of us are not living in the present. We spend the majority of our lives either in the past (if only …) or in the future (what if …). Our real power over fear, however, is right here, right now, in the present.

My journey through fear of what might be is an ongoing one. I rather suspect that I am not alone. I took a class years ago in which the instructor invited us to take our fears to its most drastic conclusion: death. For example, if I were afraid I wouldn't get an A in the class, what would be the result? The full death scenario went like this.

> Well, if I don't get an A, my status as a straight-A student is shot. This failure means I won't be valedictorian of my class. Someday, when I write a résumé, I will have to show I am not the ninth wonder of the world. I may never get a job

when the world finds out I am less than perfect. I could starve. If I starve, I could die. Dang, I better work harder on the A as this is now a matter of life or death.

The instructor soon had us all in hysterics as we saw just how silly most fears are. I don't remember the class, the instructor, or if it was my undergraduate or postgraduate degree. What I remember is the lesson. The truth is that most of our fears are quickly forgotten when the moment passes. Using the exercise above to take a situation to its most extreme is a good one to help put any fear we might have into a more rational context.

Some fear is necessary to protect us from the dangers of life and keep us alive. We need a healthy, respectful fear of getting hit by a car when crossing the street. That fear makes us look both directions. The fears I refer to in this chapter are the limiting belief fears we create that keep us from reaching our full potentials.

As a bit of levity on a serious subject, I want to add that a respectful fear of traffic is indeed necessary except in two places in the world. The first is Naples, Italy, where steady patience is the requirement. Neapolitans are the most unusual drivers in the world. Open space, regardless of where, is open game for driving. This includes sidewalks, garden paths, and the expressways. It doesn't matter if one is on a horse, scooter, or riding lawn mower. To cross a street there, you need just a little bit of space and the courage of a lion. Then you step out into the crowded street and walk at a steady pace to cross. Neapolitans will drive around you. Run, and you get run over.

Crossing a street in Turkey is very much the same, although there you need unshakable faith that you will make it. Running is required as the Turkish drivers are a tad more aggressive. As there are terrific food stands and bazaars on both sides of the streets in the big Turkish cities, the Russian roulette required to cross their streets is totally worth it!

Having said that, let me get back to our fears. I have often wondered why I can't just eliminate those irrational fears in the first place? Why do I have to be afraid of failure? Why do I have to be afraid of success? Perhaps fears are actually a form of discernment to help us all make wiser decisions. If that is true, we ought to be able to let go of fear once we decide on a particular course of action. I didn't let go of my fearful belief that I needed to work harder than everyone else (and struggle while doing it) to prove my worth and be liked. I clung to that belief for decades. The reason was simple. I didn't know I had those beliefs.

I was so busy struggling that I never questioned why. Once I started to dig into my worth from a personal perspective through my spiritual practice, I unlocked a Pandora's box of possibilities offering me the opportunity to question my perspective. Ultimately, I changed the way I question everything to a more appreciative and positive point of view, which made all the difference. I am still confronted with what-ifs, and that's okay. I now look at them from the point of positive curiosity and playful imagination. What-if can be a great way to start an empowering visualization practice!

In looking at this topic, as with all the others in this book, I look at it from my point of view. I always wanted to be liked and accepted, so my actions have frequently revolved around what other people would think of me. I wanted to be pretty and looked on with admiration, so I copied others' styles, which usually didn't suit me. I wanted to be enough or even more than enough in every situation, so I worked harder than most. I always wanted to be noticed. The promotions and awards didn't register with me as recognition because I still didn't believe in myself. A few years ago, I came to realize that the world would never see me any differently until I learned to see myself differently. By focusing and improving my self-view, my now positive choices guide me and make me better able to interact with the world in a healthy way.

Fortunately, there is a plethora of wonderful resources to help us heal our fears and unleash our potentials. One of the books that greatly influenced me was *Heal Your Life* by Louise Hay. The book is all about healing your life through self-love and positive affirmations. She writes, "Your relationship with people, things, and food is a direct reflection of your relationship with yourself."

That phrase had a big impact on me. As I am studying so many self-affirming practices, I am coming to understand that I am not just okay; rather, I am magnificent, as are all people. Somewhere in the course of life, many people come to believe they are less than [fill in the blank], and this point of view changes how they look at everything. The less-than point of view becomes a filter through which we see the world.

We must somehow get past the notion that we are not good enough. "Good enough for what?" you ask. Exactly! As I have taken a more positive view of who I am—magnificent—my view of everything is so much more illuminated. I can look at positive and negative events and see some value if only for the opportunity to grow. I must say I prefer the positive over the negative, but the negative offers me an opportunity to become greater than I was before. I can choose resentment, fear, jealousy, and guilt. Or I can choose love, forgiveness, inclusion, and grace.

There is always a choice in how I respond. There is always a choice in the meaning I give an event. Making a healthy mental or physical choice is a practice that never really goes away. It is a practice of staying in this moment, right here and right now. This moment is where our true power lies. Making the shift to a more positive stance requires me to examine the questions I ask myself. Here are some questions that could help you understand your self-view better.

Questions to Ponder

Consider what questions you ask yourself when approaching a possibility. Is your focus on past experience as a guide? Are your what-ifs negative or positive? Do you have a fear of success?

_____

_____

_____

_____

_____

When you look in a mirror, do you see yourself as magnificent and worthy?

_____

_____

_____

_____

_____

Can you look yourself in the eyes and say out loud with real conviction that you love yourself?

_____

_____

_____

_____

_____

Are you grateful for how you were made?

_____

_____

_____

_____

_____

CHAPTER 10

Sharing My Experience

I love going to workshops and seminars. Fortunately, I have had many opportunities to attend a wide variety of them over the years. I am attracted to teachers and events in the self-development, self-empowerment, and self-improvement categories. You will note these all start with "self." For the unenlightened among us, that means you must actually do work to achieve any growth.

I cannot tell you how many times I came home from some lively event with enough enthusiasm to rival Wonder Woman only to fall back into the day-to-day stresses with a newfound sense of frustration because I couldn't do everything I learned. Admittedly, part of the problem is that I am a sucker for the vendor tables. I would have to expand my suitcases to accommodate all my newly acquired books, CDs, and DVDs, along with posters, little motivational figurines, and, of course, cute yoga outfits.

News flash reminder: Cute yoga outfits do not a yogi make! I recently heard a young entrepreneur speak. He is a twenty-year-old kid named Simon, who was making more money than the average fifty-year-old. When asked what his secret was, he said that we are surrounded by so much great information but lack implementation. Talk about hitting me where it hurts. Before I beat myself up in shame that I am a workshop junkie, I must remember that every event I attended helped me grow a little. In some cases, quite a lot! However, some of the books I purchased I didn't read for years. I did listen to most of the DVDs and CDs because listening is sometimes easier than reading.

What I have come to understand is that each event I was drawn to planted seeds that initiated changes in my life. In some cases, the seed was a person I met. In some cases, it was a concept I learned. And sometimes, it was the impetus I needed to make a life change. Most of the shelved books have been read by now. What is interesting is the timing and circumstances of when I finally read a particular book. It was almost as if the universe showed me the book I needed at exactly the time I needed it.

For example, I received a free book at a workshop I went to in 2013 titled *Breadcrumbs for Beginners: Following the Writing Trail* by Dr. Sherry L. Meinberg. My swag bag was already full, so I tossed the book into the bag and forgot about it. When I got home, I simply put it on a shelf. In 2017, I started writing this book and didn't know how to go about it. A few months later, I chose that free book for my next read only to discover it is an informational book for people who want to become writers. Universal timing is pretty amazing.

The impetus driving me to write this book is that for whatever reason my higher power has, I have had an interesting and diverse life. As I began my journey to self-love, happiness, and beauty, I had the opportunity to learn through books, seminars, teachers, and practice. I had the financial means to pay for coaches and travel for workshops. I bent a few credit cards buying books, which I eventually read. Along the way, I have learned and transformed.

What I have come to realize is that I am indeed fortunate. When I go to a seminar, there might be a thousand people there, or perhaps only three hundred. That is such a small number compared to the thousands who live day to day, wondering how they are surviving and feeling deflated about themselves.

I was a leader and mentor for many years, always helping others grow and succeed without nurturing my soul. Because

I was a leader in a frequently male-dominated environment, I found myself hiding my feminine core behind a masculine mask, all while struggling to feel worthy. Unfortunately, many women leaders and managers still feel the need to hide their true feminine core in order to get ahead. I understand this dilemma so clearly, especially due to the years I spent in the military because I was frequently the only female officer in a roomful of men.

I believe this situation is slowly changing, however. And I want to help women and men understand that whatever role they are in, it is so important and necessary to stay true to our basic natures and authentic selves. This change in perspective will take time as women learn to be strong and feminine, and men learn to celebrate both qualities.

As my heart opened, I noticed people seemed to gravitate naturally toward me, seeking answers. They needed to hear they are special, wonderful, and yes, beautiful. I now realize we all are meant to share our knowledge. In the past, generations of families lived together. The elders taught the younger through their stories. There was a living example of how connection and love happened.

Somewhere in our modern world, the norm changed. We were encouraged to go out on our own. People became more separate and alienated from each other. Like hamsters on a wheel, we are caught in a race that has no end. It is demoralizing. Our souls are crying to get off the wheel and get connected to others. In the back of our minds, we are looking for peace of mind and someone to give us answers as to what it all means. We need to find meaning and purpose. Perhaps that is what drew me to so many seminars.

I sought teachers in books, seminars, and coaching sessions. What I understand now is that teachers abound. In fact, they are all around us in many forms—from nature itself to inspired thought from within. The trick is to stay present and see what there is to learn. The first step in any personal transformation is to remove yourself from the role of victim (hamster/wheel) in which you see life happening to you. For example, when you focus on excuses such as a sorry job, a dysfunctional family, a tough upbringing, or scary relationship, you will remain in the backseat as a victim.

However, you have the power to change that role to one of life learner, adventurer even, by taking back your power in any situation. The power is a shift in perspective. I can hear you now … "Great, Kari, and just how am I supposed to do that?"

It starts by being present enough to see what is really happening. If you focus on why something happened that led to your current situation, you are hanging out in the past and trying to find blame. If you focus on how it will be different when you get out of your current situation, you are hanging out in the future. What that leaves is the present. It is in the present that you have a choice to change your perception of what is happening. Staying in the present is a moment-by-moment practice. You get there by bringing your awareness to what is happening right now. Step 1 is to change your focus from the past or future, and plant it firmly in the now.

Step 2 in changing your perspective is to take personal responsibility for your now. It is so easy to look to others for blame if something isn't going well. I blamed my family upbringing for making me feel invisible. I blamed a well-meaning teacher for making me feel less than smart. I can go on, but I think you get the picture. It was when I began to question the validity of my limiting beliefs that I could start the process of letting blame go. As I did, I could do the work to put the light of truth on the offending belief and change it for good once and for all.

I had to take responsibility for what was happening rather than blame people or situations for my circumstances and the meaning I gave them.

Step 3 is to look hard at what meaning you give something or some situation to determine if the meaning is true. This lens of perspective requires a deep dive into our beliefs. I use my roller-coaster journey with my weight and weight loss as an example of all three steps. I haven't covered this in the book, but like many people, I struggle with my weight. Steps 1 and 2 were to stop looking at past failures or my perception of what caused my weight issues—placing blame—which, of course, is hanging out in the past. I also had to stop the story that when I lose weight, everything will improve, which is hanging out in the future. Instead, I had to look at where I am today, just as I am today.

In case you are wondering, this shift to a more-present perspective takes practice. Indeed, it is an ongoing exercise. Practicing present perspective in any given situation is good because the shift will flow eventually into all areas of your life.

Step 3 was to look at what assumptions and meaning I gave to my weight. I used to associate likability with waist size. Now I know my desire to lose weight is more health-related versus a relationship requirement. We have a much better chance of learning to love ourselves in the present as well. The past can lead to blame and the future to fantasy. The present is inviting and a great place to begin your journey of self-love.

I approached my weight management journey by looking at how I felt about myself. Did extra weight make me less lovable? Did it change the way people viewed me or their friendships with me? As with any issue or problem, I guarantee we have limiting beliefs around the issue if we have yet to change it. For me, I blurred the line between my limiting beliefs and my tried-and-true story of why I am overweight.

I told myself for years that I was big-boned and built like a linebacker, which isn't true. All my life, I had been told we were good German peasant stock or had the family linebacker build because my grandfather was a big man. Not fat, just big like a linebacker. I also believed my work situation or the craziness around my lunchtime was at fault. I believed, at least on some level, that there was nothing I could do about it.

I had to look at my limiting beliefs and break them down. Were they true? There is frequently some element of truth to the stories we tell ourselves. It is important to look at those elements, but then, at least for me, I had to stop looking at them and take personal responsibility for my health. I had to decide what I wanted for me. No one else could make this decision. No one can make it for you either.

When I embraced responsibility for my health [fill in the blank for yourself if health is not an issue], I started to make real changes in my life. I went through a roller coaster of emotions along the way. There was an element of shame that I had allowed myself to gain so much weight. When we get off the blame game and start taking personal responsibility, that action puts our failures right back in our faces. It is critical to let go of judgment right here and right now. We are where we are. It does not define us! It is not who we are! Reread that a few times.

Where we are is nothing more than a starting point for where we want to be. I took stock of the situation and made some decisions about what and how I wanted to change it. Next—and this is so important—I came to a place of gratitude for exactly where I was. By coming back to the present and endeavoring to stay there, I realized I was learning valuable lessons and growing as a human being. I also realized during this time that I could pass on the wisdom of my life's lessons and perhaps uplift another individual who was ready to take his or her life to the next level. Now might be an appropriate time for another quote.

> Love the life you have while you create the life
> that you want. Don't think you have to choose
> one over the other. (Hal Elrod)

Another side effect of taking personal responsibility without judgment is that in these moments, we can begin to heal the effects of our past and make room for our wonderful now and whatever future we want to create.

The more I dug into my own limiting beliefs and blame patterns, the more I knew I wanted to share my story with others. As I mentioned before, I am not a rock star or athlete. I am, however, another traveler on this journey called life. I have had numerous wonderful adventures and plenty of bumps and bruises too.

For whatever reason, I have had opportunities and access to great teachers. And when I started trying out new ideas for myself, some worked, and some were not for me. But I realized that if I can share where my journey took me from and where I feel like I am now, it might help another person along the way. People tell me I glow now because I am happy. When I ask if they love themselves, many cannot even respond. There is instant emotion. I have met many people who cannot say, "Hello, gorgeous," when looking in a mirror. They simply don't believe it.

My theory is that if we all learn to love ourselves, we will become inherently happy, and that has to affect the world around us. This self-love will most certainly up our beauty quotient. At the beginning of this book, I mentioned that when we are happy, people perceive us as beautiful regardless of our actual physical appearance. Our beauty comes from the glow of self-love and happiness. My deep desire is to help everyone who reads this find that beauty.

Questions to Ponder

Examine your current situation. What is an issue you have with yourself or your environment? Please do this without judgment as this is an exercise to help you.

_____

_____

_____

_____

_____

Really look at this situation. What are your limiting beliefs around it? Are you viewing if from the past or the future?

_____

_____

_____

_____

_____

Is there a lesson to learn from this situation?

_____

_____

_____

_____

_____

What silver lining can you find to this situation, something for which you can be grateful?

_____

_____

_____

_____

_____

Action: Go to the nearest mirror and look deep in to your eyes. Smile and say out loud, "Hello, gorgeous." Another powerful statement to make in front of a mirror is to state your name out loud and say, "I love you."

_____

_____

_____

_____

_____

CHAPTER 11

The Journey Begins

I have always enjoyed learning—even when I didn't think I was smart. In fact, I love to take noncredited courses at universities and community colleges. I think learning is a part of who we are, and if we are not continually learning, we are surely going backward. I started a whole new type of learning later in life, post college as it were. That learning was my spiritual path. Remember, a spiritual path is not a religious thing, and there's no dogma behind it. It is looking inside and asking those basic questions we all ask eventually, such as, what is my purpose here? Am I of value, or am I contributing value? Are my beliefs still valid? Do I have something more to say? Who's answering all the questions anyway?

A spiritual journey is much more about what's going on inside than what is going on outside. However, this internal exploration absolutely affects the external journey. I found that as I started answering these questions, I began to clear the fog that obscured my vision of who I truly am. In the light of my truth, I began to see and feel my beauty. The path to this feeling is lit now by my inner light, and it is wonderful. The thing is that a feeling of self-love is not a destination to arrive at but a lifelong journey to become our best versions of ourselves every day.

You see, one does not wake up and say, "I think I'll enter

into my spiritual journey now." No, the universe actually gives us gentle nudges throughout our lives, perhaps in the form of a book, a blog, something someone says, or even a song lyric that sets us to thinking about something more than our mundane day-to-day lives.

Earlier I mentioned that you probably heard that when the student is ready, the teacher will come. For some people, the teacher shows up early in life. For me, not so much. Somewhere midlife or so, I became curious about so many things, such as Tarot, crop circles, energy healing, and even the origins of the Bible. I began to question my beliefs and deeply explore what made me believe what I believed about my possibilities in life. I was not particularly happy at that period of my life, and the exploration into the bigger picture of my reality seemed a nice diversion.

I now know this inner exploration was the beginning of finding peace in whatever my current life situation was. It is in this peace that I find my inner beauty, and this translates to outer beauty. The first step to finding inner beauty and strength is to love yourself. It takes work to get rid of all that prevents self-love. The path of self-exploration is not without bumps in the road, and that is okay. Remember the analogy of the roller coaster?

Those bumps can be opportunities with a shift in perspective from, "Why me?" to "What is there for me to learn in this situation?" It is important to develop curiosity about what holds you back from your true potential without the habitual judgment that tends to rear its ugly head when deep diving in self-exploration.

Some of the things that made me curious caused great concern for my family as these explorations went outside our fairly normal Christian parameters. However, what I've found in this now lifelong journey is that there is love, a foundational essence that drives all things in our lives. I understand my journey is really about learning to listen to that love and to find wisdom in that essence. The love is always there, offering opportunities for love, gratitude, forgiveness, understanding, and compassion. Rest assured, seeing the opportunities in a time of great stress, abuse, anger, or hurt is hard. At times, it's almost impossible. The trick is to stay present and keep looking for the lesson.

One of my favorite quotes comes from Dewitt James, a photographer for *National Geographic.* He says, "We always have the option to reframe obstacles into opportunities." Doing that reframing takes practice, but I contend the results are worth the effort.

The first thing I always do when I get lost in negative events or emotions is to look for anything for which I can find gratitude. Anything, regardless of how small. It could be something as simple as finding gratitude I can breathe through my anger. And with slow, deep, controlled breaths, I can calm myself. That is surely worth my gratitude. In this new calmer state, I can begin to see everything clearer.

In this calmer state, I can determine my choices in the situation and make the choices that will uplift me and serve my highest good. The more I practice finding gratitude and whatever the universe is trying to teach me, the happier I have become. It also seems the more I express gratitude, the more things come into my experience for which I can be grateful. It reminds me of something Dr. Wayne Dwyer used to say. He said, "When we change the way we look at things, the things we look at will change."

I now want to share what I am learning because I can say rather emphatically, that being happy is much better than living in the shadow of doubt and self-judgment.

Speaking of Dr. Dwyer, several years ago I heard him speak at a Hay House Publishing event titled "I Can Do It." As I listened to his wisdom, I initially thought he was only repeating quotes and bits of information from other books and authors such as Eckhart Tolle and Rumi. Dr. Dwyer loved to regale audiences with interesting and timely quotes. However, it occurred to me that what he had actually done was take that knowledge and apply it to his life situation before sharing with the audience the new wisdom derived from his experiences. All of us in the room listened with rapt attention.

Of course, this is exactly what teaching is. Good teachers recycle and enhance what they have learned and apply it to their own life experiences. They pass on the wisdom derived from incorporating that learning into their expressions of life. I have come to believe it is our responsibility to share what we learn to help serve others on their paths.

With that in mind, I decided to write this book, which is really what I've learned and how I applied it to my life. I hope there were some pearls of wisdom that will help you along your spiritual path. My deepest wish, however, is that every person who reads this book will find their happy places and move into their beauty from there. I believe in you and your magnificence.

As I continue my exploration, I realize I want to help my fellow travelers in life step into their power, beauty, and inner peace. You see, all my experiences have led me to an understanding that took me from a place of not enough and fear to one of beauty, strength, power, happiness, and joyful radiance.

I discovered that happiness is not a destination I was aiming for but rather, a state of being in which I choose to live. Part 2 of that discovery is that I was the only one holding me back.

Getting to where I actively make that choice every day is really what my journey is all about. For most of us, our first choice is frequently doubt, fear, smallness, or some other diminishing emotion instead of letting our true lights shine. Perhaps as you have read about my experiences, you learned that you have a choice to be happy and therefore beautiful. We are all beautiful, magnificent creations of God. Marianne Williamson's quote sums this concept up so beautifully.

Our deepest fear is not that we are inadequate. Our deepest fear is that we are powerful beyond measure. It is our light, not our darkness that most frightens us. We ask ourselves, "Who am I to be brilliant, gorgeous, talented, fabulous?" Actually, who are you not to be? You are a child of God. You playing small does not serve the world. There is nothing enlightened about shrinking so that other people won't feel insecure around you. We are all meant to shine, as children do. We were born to make manifest the glory of God that is within us. It's not just in some of us; it's for everyone. And as we let our light shine, we unconsciously permit other people to do the same. As we liberate ourselves from our fear, our presence automatically liberates others.

Now it is your turn. Can you be brave enough to ask tough questions about your limiting beliefs? Are you ready to start loving yourself just as you are today? Can you embrace your choices to find gratitude for every bump in the road and learn from them? It is sometimes very easy to do. Other times, you will have to dig deep to change lifelong negative patterns. But I promise you it is worth it. If you start this path toward being truly happy, your life will change. Some of that change will only be a shift in perspective, with little apparent external change. That is okay as sometimes it is all that is necessary.

However, my experiences showed me that as I let go of limiting beliefs and fears, some people in my life began to push back. They recognized my liberation, and it was threatening to them because they were still stuck in fear. One of two things will happen in this situation. The first is that your newfound light will draw them in like a moth to a flame, and they will want what you have. If that is the case, please spread the news! Have the courage to share your story. Encourage them that letting go of fear and loving themselves will enrich them. Become the next teacher even as you keep learning.

The other scenario is that those stuck in fear will become even more fearful and push back. These people may say you are being selfish or question your motives; like taking care of yourself is somehow wrong. You might even hear questions about whether you have joined a cult or something crazy like that. You cannot remove their fears. Only they can.

Hang on with all your might to your inner joy and love. They are your precious gifts to yourself. How you were created by God/the universe/Spirit is worth celebrating. We are meant to be fulfilled and happy.

With that in mind, lovingly and compassionately let these fearful people go out of your life. Trust that as you release people, places, and beliefs that don't serve you any longer, you clear out space for light, love, and amazing people and experiences to come into your life. I am not asking you to tell a lifelong friend or a family member that you can no longer associate with them. That would be silly. I only encourage you to spend less time with them and seek friendships that are uplifting and empowering. Jim Rohn states that you are the average of the five people you spend the most time with, so surround yourself with people who are going to help you become the best version of yourself. They should be your champions, cheerleaders, teachers, and partners in creating a magnificent life.

Today, I can and do look in mirrors with a smile. I greet myself with a happy, "Hello, gorgeous," and invite myself to have a good day. Most days, I do just that. On the days that I hit a wall or feel frumpy, I find compassion for myself and rest if needed or dig deeper to find the cause of my malaise. I may not feel better once I discover what is bugging me, but knowledge is liberating. Or perhaps I should say illuminating. I can face myself in this light and make a new choice. As a friend and colleague said to me once, there are no good or bad days. There are only good and better days. It is a shift in perspective, my friends.

My desire is that you will begin to shift your perception of yourself from not enough to magnificent. I hope you find the courage to begin loving yourself and honoring every unique thing about you.

I end with a quote from Father Richard Rohr, a Franciscan priest. He was writing on the teachings of another Franciscan-style philosopher-theologian, Jon Duns Scotus (1265/66–1308). What he wrote touched me so deeply because when I read it, I knew I could not belittle myself anymore. I couldn't play small one more day. I knew I was special.

> The absolute freedom of God allows God to create, or not to create, each creature. Its existence means God has positively chosen to create that creature, precisely as it is … Each individual act of creation is a once-in-eternity choice on God's part.

You are special. You are loved. You are beautiful.

Question to Ponder

Do you believe it?

_____

_____

_____

_____

_____

EPILOGUE

Writing a book is an interesting process. Starting to write was easier than I thought. I had been mentoring and coaching people for some time. All I had to do was start putting my thoughts on paper. As I wrote, however, I found myself digging deeper into those thoughts to determine if I only imagined some of my experiences. That sounds silly, but when trying to recall events from more than fifty years ago, I wanted to make sure I was not inventing situations based on my now-fading childhood perceptions.

This book is my deeply personal story. But my life did not happen in a bubble. I was surrounded by family, colleagues, and friends. As I wrote, I had to consider how what I had to say might affect them. I left out names and tried to be respectful in all my stories. This concern for others' feelings was especially true for my sister and mother.

You see, I currently share a home with both of them. As they lived in the same household I describe, it was intimidating to write about how I perceived my childhood homelife while sharing my current life situation with them. What if they didn't appreciate my approach? What if they didn't agree with what I wrote? Those dreaded what-ifs still percolate to the surface ever so often.

For several months, I wrote without sharing anything I put to paper with them. I was intimidated by the thought of them reading my words. Fear, it would seem, still lurks beneath the surface. Finally, I started to share the book with my sister. She didn't particularly like parts of it, which made me get defensive. For a few days, we had a bit of tension in the house.

I believe part of my healing process has been to openly discuss how I felt about the events that occurred in my family life. I did so without blame because that is not the point of this story. Freeing myself from blame and sliding into a healthier relationship with everyone around me, including me, is the entire object of the book. I finally listened to my sister and learned about some of her perceptions as well. I believe being willing to hear her out on why she didn't like parts of it helped me approach our current life situation with a more open heart.

Showing my mom was the hard part. I didn't want her to feel like she failed me. It took tremendous courage to sit down with her and show her the first few chapters of the book. She surprised me, however. She understood what I was trying to accomplish with the telling of her part of the story. She helped me correct a few things I had wrong (it was a long time ago), particularly in the family backdrop portion. Sections of that referenced the time before I was born. We had some meaningful conversations that continue to this day. I am grateful I decided to write my story, but I am most grateful that I took the chance to share it with my family.

How you approach letting go of limiting beliefs is entirely up to you. I encourage you to be compassionate with anyone who inadvertently helped you create them in the first place. You may even choose to keep your exploration to yourself. But I encourage you to find people, however, who can help uplift you while you unravel the net that might be holding you back from your potential. Should you choose to write your story, be assured it will change your life!

I wish you freedom from fear and that you find joy in all you do.

GRATITUDE

There are many people to thank in my life. People who have helped me become the woman I am today through our combined life experiences. My mom and dad played pivotal roles in my life, although it took me some time to see that. I am grateful to my father for encouraging my military career. I am grateful to my mother for always trying to do the right thing and for her generous heart. I am blessed beyond belief for the support and love of my sister. We share a special bond, and my life is richer for it.

I am grateful for Hal Elrod and the community of people he brought together through The Miracle Morning. They are positive, uplifting, and changing the world to become a better place one morning at a time.

I am grateful for Mike Lonzetta, my first coach. With a gentle heart and wisdom beyond his years, he helped me overcome so many fears. I now have a few different coaches who assist me. If you have not taken advantage of what a coach has to offer, I strongly encourage your to seek out someone to help you shorten the distance between where you are to where you want to be.

I am grateful to Cassidy and Ryan Bones, who helped me in more ways than I can count. They were my first coaching clients, and I was the first client for their consulting business, Ascension Consulting. We are friends coming together to uplift and create magical lives.

So many people have helped me become happy, and I am

grateful to them all. Finally, I am grateful to you, the reader. I am so happy that you decided to invest in yourself. You are worth it.

For more information, please join me at my www.conquerlifecoaching.com or find me at www.facebook.com/conquerlifecoaching.

ABOUT THE AUTHOR

Kari Romeo's career path took her down many different avenues. She is a retired Air Force officer, has managed numerous retail stores and is presently a Real Estate agent as well as a transformational life coach. To the outside observer, she appeared to be a highly successful woman. In her mind, however, she struggled with a lack of self-esteem, questioning her worth, and feeling like she just wasn't enough. Kari struggled to feel feminine while wearing a more masculine mask she felt was needed to be successful in leadership positions. Kari realized that limiting beliefs were robbing her of her potential, her opportunities, and her joy. She took up the challenge to eliminate these damaging beliefs to unlock her happiness. Using the power of questions to find her truth, Kari freed herself from a lifetime of self-criticism and judgment. She removed her habitual negative cloak and learned to embrace her inner light. Now it is her passion to help others embrace themselves with love, joy, and compassion so they too, may be free to shine beautifully!

For more information on Kari's coaching programs or to watch her TEDx Coeur d'Alene talk entitled Teaching The Inner Critic A New Story, please visit www.conquerlifecoaching.com